Tackling TULIP

Exposing the Biblical, Theological, and Practical Errors of Calvinism

Grant Ralston and Edward Ralston

WESTBOW
PRESS®
A DIVISION OF THOMAS NELSON
& ZONDERVAN

WestBow Press books may be ordered through booksellers or by contacting:

WestBow Press
A Division of Thomas Nelson & Zondervan
1663 Liberty Drive
Bloomington, IN 47403
www.westbowpress.com
1 (866) 928-1240

Scripture quotations are taken from the King James Version of the Bible.

ISBN: 978-1-9736-6809-1 (sc)
ISBN: 978-1-9736-6811-4 (hc)
ISBN: 978-1-9736-6810-7 (e)

Library of Congress Control Number: 2019908958

Print information available on the last page.

WestBow Press rev. date: 7/24/2019

CONTENTS

FOREWORD

"Whosoever Will" or "A Whosoever Gospel"

Mat 16:25 *"For **whosoever** will save his life shall lose it: and **whosoever** will lose his life for my sake shall find it."*

Rom 10:13 *"For **whosoever** shall call upon the name of the Lord shall be saved."*

John 3:16 *"For God so loved the world, that he gave his only begotten Son, that **whosoever** believeth in him should not perish, but have everlasting life."*

J.H. Jowett trained preachers to articulate their entire sermon in one sentence. He felt the sermon couldn't be constructed or articulated correctly until that sentence had been written. It is hard to imagine a sermon being able to be reduced to a single sentence, but it is true and very effective. The same practice could be applied to a book, lecture, or even a college class. What is the essence or big idea of what is being taught? If *Tackling TULIP* was boiled down to one sentence, I believe that sentence would be this: **The gospel of Jesus Christ is for whosoever will!**

The conviction that the gospel is for whosoever has come under greater attack in the American church in recent decades. Those who oppose the idea of a whosoever gospel believe that God has already selected who will be saved, and it has already been determined. The adherents of this doctrine are usually known as Calvinists or, more recently, have become known as followers of Reformed theology. Justin Taylor in 2012 shared 10 reasons why Mark Dever believes that Reformed theology has seen a resurgence in recent years. Adding to Dever's list, Taylor adds the role that Christian publishing has played in the aiding of this growth. I agree with his insight. *Tackling TULIP* is an attempt to publish a concise biblical account of salvation that answers the false teachings of Reformed theology.

I know the authors of this book, and it was not written in condescending arrogance or shallow emotionalism, but rather a deep and broad presentation of the full gospel of Jesus Christ. It is not a mere rebuttal of a few isolated passages of Scripture Reformed theologians twist, but a full account of God's revealed word concerning the good news for whosoever. The authors have presented a comprehensive account of the Scriptures that will help you understand salvation more completely. The authors (Rev. Ed Ralston and Rev. Grant Ralston) are a grandfather/grandson team! It is a privilege to watch my father and son work together on this important project.

I hope you will take the time to read *Tackling TULIP* for several reasons. First, I believe this book may be the most important book you will ever read because it deals with our salvation! Whether you are a young person in college, a studious pastor, or a follower of Christ growing in grace, I believe this book will be an invaluable tool for you. This book will become a reference for you for years to come.

Second, Reformed theology limits salvation to a few based on their perception of God's arbitrary decision, leads to a life void of sanctification, and stops believers from seeking to live an empowered, Spirit-filled life. This doctrine has affected people I love, and it needs to be answered fully and completely.

Third, I have encouraged this generation to write books, lessons, and sermons to defend our theological positions. Many Calvinists have interpreted our lack of printed materials as a sign there is no answer to their theological positions. Nothing could be further from the truth, and *Tackling TULIP* is an answer to my prayers that this generation will produce more of this quality of work.

I was in Brazil earlier this year on a missionary trip and watched our team preach to thousands of people we had never met. What a joy it is to be able to preach the gospel and declare, "God wants to save you" or "come to Jesus tonight to be saved." If I didn't believe the gospel was a whosoever gospel, I wouldn't be able to make those statements in sincerity or honesty. But I believe the Bible presents the heart of God pursuing all lost humanity with utmost abandonment! I believe God presented a "whosoever-will" gospel!

Dr. Ryan E. Ralston, President
Heritage Bible College

INTRODUCTION

Nobody becomes a Calvinist through his own reading of the Bible. He must be introduced to Calvinism in order to see it in the Bible. He did not arrive at Calvinism through an independent, thorough study of the Scriptures. On the contrary, he had to be "taught" it, first, before he could see it in the word of God. That it is necessary to learn Calvinism before finding it in the Bible can be confirmed by examining the writings of John Calvin, the French Reformer who systematized these doctrines that later bore his name. He wrote a highly influential book, *Institutes of the Christian Religion*. In the preface to the reader of his 1539 edition, Calvin makes some interesting statements:

> My object in this work was to prepare and train students of theology for the study of the sacred volume, so that they might both have an easy introduction to it, and be able to proceed in it, with unfaltering step, seeing I have endeavored to give such a summary of religion in all its parts, and have digested it into such an order as may *make it not difficult for any one, who is rightly acquainted with it, to ascertain both what he ought principally to look for in Scripture*, and also to what head he ought to refer whatever is contained in it. Having thus, as it were, paved the way, I shall not feel it necessary, in any commentaries on Scripture which I may afterward

publish, to enter into long discussions of doctrine or dilate on common-places, and will, therefore, always compress them. In this way the pious reader will be saved much trouble and weariness, *provided he comes furnished with a knowledge of the present work as an essential prerequisite.*[1]

Calvin boldly declares this work designed to "train students of theology for the study of the sacred volume" will make it easy for anyone to "ascertain ... what he ought principally to look for in Scripture." Someone "furnished with a knowledge of the present work as an essential prerequisite" will not have to exert much time and energy into studying other areas of doctrine. In other words, Calvin wants his readers to just trust him, no questions asked, and once they accept what he says in the *Institutes*, they will know what they should look for and what to believe about the Scriptures.

Furthermore, Calvin, in the preface to the first French edition of the *Institutes*, published in 1545, maintains a similar perspective. He writes:

> I dare not bear too strong a testimony in its favor, and declare how profitable the reading of it will be, lest I should seem to prize my own work too highly. However, I may promise this much, that it will be a kind of key opening up to all the children of God a right and ready access to the understanding of the sacred volume ... Since we are bound to acknowledge that all truth and sound doctrine proceed from God, I will venture boldly to declare what I think of this work, acknowledging it to be God's work rather than mine.[2]

---

[1] John Calvin, *Institutes of the Christian Religion* (Peabody: Hendrickson Publishers, 2008), xxxiv. Italics mine.

[2] Ibid., xxxv.

Clearly, Calvin thought rather highly of his book on theology. He believed that it would be "a kind of key" that would provide greater access into understanding "the sacred volume." To put it another way, in order to truly grasp what the Scriptures are trying to teach, it is necessary to become acquainted with Calvin's work, and once you have become aware of what you ought to principally look for in Scripture, you would then have ready access to the Bible and be able to comprehend it correctly.

While modern Calvinists probably would not admit the necessity of learning Calvinism before reading it in the Bible, it does seem to be a logical inference from Calvin's own words. Nevertheless, whether a Calvinist admits it does not negate our contention that a simple, objective reading of the Scriptures does not lead to Calvinism. A person becomes a Calvinist because he learned it elsewhere and adopted the theological presuppositions, not because he prayerfully studied the Bible apart from any excessive influences.

Perhaps, you are unfamiliar with John Calvin and the theological system that bears his name. You have heard the term 'Calvinism' mentioned before, but your grasp on its essential tenets is fuzzy. What exactly is Calvinism? Calvinism is often summarized by the acrostic TULIP. TULIP stands for:

❖ Total depravity. This doctrine stresses that the effects of the fall make it impossible for human beings to choose Christ apart from God's sovereign work of regeneration. Fallen men and women are spiritually dead, like a corpse, and cannot respond positively to God's gracious attempts to reconcile them.

❖ Unconditional election. Before the creation of the world, God chose a particular group of people, named the elect, for eternal salvation. The corollary to his choice of some for salvation is that, in sorrow, he passed over those he did not choose. The reason God chose some and not others (or all) is not because of any foreseen faith or good works but simply because of his sovereign good pleasure.

❖ Limited atonement. Christ died only for the elect. He did not die for everyone. According to the Calvinist, it would have been an abject failure on Christ's part to die for someone who would die lost and spend eternity in hell. Therefore, everyone for whom Christ died will be saved because he accomplished their salvation through his atoning work.

❖ Irresistible grace. When God decides to save a person, there is no force in the entire universe that can resist his will, including the will of the individual who is being saved. Once God changes the disposition of a human heart, he will come to Christ because that is what he now wants to do. Before God sovereignly regenerates him, however, he never would have come to Christ because he hated God, as all unregenerate persons do.

❖ Perseverance of the Saints. Those whom God has truly saved will necessarily persevere until the end of their lives. Any professing Christian who falls away before the finish line was never saved in the first place. Anyone born of God will never fall away because God will preserve them and bring their salvation to completion.

These five doctrines encapsulate much of what Reformed theology[3] teaches. Although there are other distinguishing features to Calvinism, TULIP is a helpful way to summarize this theological system. Throughout this book, it will be our aim to demonstrate why Calvinism is erroneous biblically, theologically, and practically. We will address TULIP as it relates to the appropriate chapter. Our prayer is that by the end of this book, you will see the threat that Calvinism poses to the church of Jesus Christ and be equipped to refute these fallacious doctrines.

---

[3] Most Calvinists use the expression "Reformed theology" interchangeably with Calvinism. Although this might not be historically accurate, to accommodate for contemporary usage, Reformed theology will be used sometimes throughout this book as a synonym for Calvinism.

PART 1

The Biblical Problems of Calvinism

CHAPTER 1

The Faithful Jews and John 6

Calvinists often appeal to isolated verses in the sixth chapter of John's gospel to support their theological system. In an effort to construct the doctrines of total depravity, unconditional election, limited atonement, irresistible grace, and the perseverance of the saints, those who subscribe to Calvinism take many passages out of context. John 6 is a frequent victim of this contextual abuse. Proper biblical interpretation must give respect to *both* the grammar and the context of the scriptures. While certain interpretations might be plausible grammatically, any understanding of a biblical passage that ignores the context is erroneous and should be dismissed by serious students of the Bible.

An egregious example of this contextual abuse committed by a Calvinist in relation to John 6 appears in R. C. Sproul's *Chosen by God*.[4] He appeals to John 6:44, which records the words of Jesus. "No man can come to me, except the Father which hath sent me draw him." Sproul proceeds to argue that "the key word here is *draw*."[5] To

---

[4] R. C. Sproul, *Chosen by God* (Carol Stream, IL: Tyndale House Publishers, 1986).

[5] Ibid., 69.

him, this word does not suggest a wooing or enticement; instead, it suggests an irresistible dragging to Christ. Sproul then refers to Kittel's *Theological Dictionary of the New Testament* and asserts that this respected authority on the Greek of the New Testament defines the Greek word used here for "draw" as "to compel by irresistible superiority."[6]

What is especially interesting is that while Sproul references Kittel's *Theological Dictionary of the New Testament*, he does not provide a citation to assist the reader in finding the location of this definition in Kittel's massive work. Perhaps the reason that he does not reveal this information is that he is afraid his readers will call his bluff. A brief look at what Kittel actually says about this Greek word, *as it is used in John 6:44*, is insightful:

> [The force of love] is the point in the two important passages in John 6:44; 12:32. There is *no thought here of force* or magic. The term figuratively expresses the supernatural power of the love of God or Christ which goes out to all (12:32) but without which no one can come (6:44). The apparent contradiction shows that both the election and the universality of grace must be taken seriously; *the compulsion is not automatic.*[7]

Later, I will explain the meaning of John 6:44 in light of its surrounding context. However, I wanted to highlight two things. First, Sproul's deceitful use of Kittel's *Theological Dictionary of the New Testament* is unacceptable. While Kittel does acknowledge that the Greek word for "draw" does imply a compelling in certain instances, he specifically states that there is "no thought of force" in John 6:44 and that "the compulsion is not automatic." By concealing this important information from his readers, Sproul has misled them.

---

[6] Ibid.

[7] Geoffrey W. Bromiley, *Theological Dictionary of the New Testament- Abridged in One Volume* (Grand Rapids, MI: William B. Eerdmans Publishing, 1985), 227. Italics mine.

Second, he also fails to consider the context of John 6. On the pages that Sproul discusses this key text, he never even attempts to explain how the drawing of the Father to Christ fits into the context. Instead, he launches into a debate over what it entails to be drawn by God to Jesus Christ. As mentioned previously, although an interpretation could be acceptable grammatically, it might be contextually inadequate. No passage of scripture stands in isolation or in opposition to the rest of God's Word. Due consideration must be given to the context of every passage in the Bible to avoid producing and spreading distortions of God's Word.

John 6 might seem to be an impenetrable fortress defending the doctrines of Calvinism. Can this passage be interpreted faithfully in a way that does not support Calvinism? Absolutely. It is our contention that *only* the blinding theological presuppositions of Calvinism will lead someone to see irresistible grace, total depravity, and the perseverance of the saints in John 6.

The Context of John 6

What is the context of John 6? One major contextual clue is John 6:38. Here, Jesus indicates that what he is teaching is primarily focused on his earthly ministry: "For I came *down from heaven*, not to do mine own will, but the will of him that sent me."[8] In this passage, Jesus is explaining what is occurring while he is "down from heaven." He is not concerned with "the notion that God has preselected a particular number of people to draw irresistibly while leaving all others without the ability to respond willingly to the revelation of God."[9] He is particularly concerned with the events that are transpiring during his incarnation.

As shocking as it may sound to some people, Jesus did not come to this earth to be a world-renowned evangelist. Throughout his

---

[8] Leighton Flowers, *The Potter's Promise* (Evansville, IN: Trinity Academic Press, 2017), 75.
[9] Ibid.

ministry, he did not seek to win thousands to faith in himself. On the contrary, repeatedly he instructed his disciples to *not* reveal that he was the Christ to anyone (Matthew 16:20; Mark 3:12). Certainly, after his resurrection, he would draw all men to himself (John 12:32), but he had a specific task to accomplish while he was "down from heaven." John 6 describes, in part, what his ministry consisted of.

Furthermore, Jesus is constantly confronted by a group of Jewish people who claimed to know God but were not coming to him in order to receive eternal life (John 5:40). According to Calvinism, the reason these Jewish people were not accepting Jesus as the Messiah is that God had withheld the necessary grace. Apparently, these Jewish people were not individually elected for salvation, so God did not draw them to Christ. This interpretation is troubling, to say the least, since it portrays God as a tyrant who demands faith and repentance, renders it impossible for those not chosen to salvation to have faith and repentance, and then punishes them with eternal damnation for not having faith and repentance even though it was literally impossible for them to have faith and repentance in Jesus Christ. Fortunately, the correct interpretation of this passage respects the free moral agency of human beings and does not paint God as a wicked and unpredictable monster whose desires contradict his decrees.

There is a principle expressed throughout the gospel of John that must be understood in order to grasp the meaning of John 6: "Rejecting God's first offerings of truth will utterly block further illumination."[10] Robert Shank agrees: "Reception of holy truth as it is offered is the indispensable prerequisite for understanding and receiving additional truth."[11] In other words, a person will not receive further revelation from God if he or she is currently rejecting the light of truth that God has already given to him or her.

This principle can be seen by observing that although the Jewish people claimed to know God, in actuality, they did not know

---

[10] Jerry L. Walls and Joseph R. Dongell, *Why I Am Not a Calvinist* (Downers Grove, IL: InterVarsity Press, 2004), 74-75.

[11] Robert Shank, *Elect in the Son* (Minneapolis, MN: Bethany House Publishers, 1989), 178.

him. Jesus explains this situation in various places throughout John's gospel. For example, he declared, "But I know you, that *ye have not the love of God in you*" (John 5:42). As a matter of fact, they did not even believe what Moses had written. "For had ye believed Moses, ye would have believed me: for he wrote of me. But if ye believe not his writings, how shall ye believe my words?" (John 5:46–47). The Jewish people, as a whole, had rejected the light of God revealed through Moses, and because they did not accept what Moses wrote, they would not accept what Christ taught. As Jesus told them later, "If God were your Father, ye would love me" (John 8:42). They gave proof that they did not really know God, for if they were truly serving God, they would have received the message of Christ. The fact that they did not receive Jesus as the one sent from the Father signified that they did not know the Father (John 7:28).

Many biblical scholars agree with the view that those who rejected Jesus did so because they had first rejected the Father. For instance, I. Howard Marshall wrote,

> When we bear in mind that the Gospel of John is addressed primarily to Jews, it seems reasonable to venture the suggestion that John is teaching that Jews who fail to accept the revelation of God which He had already given before the coming of Jesus cannot hope to bypass it and come to Jesus in some other way. Put otherwise, the reason why the Jews failed to believe in Jesus was because they had already failed to believe in the earlier revelations of God to them ... A Jew, then, who had already refused the word of God given to him in the Scriptures would not believe the new revelation given in Jesus (Luke 16:31).[12]

---

[12] I. Howard Marshall, *Kept by the Power of God* (Eugene, OR: Wipf & Stock Publishers, 2007), 179-180.

This excellent insight from Marshall is reinforced by W. Purkiser, Richard Taylor, and Willard Taylor. In their book *God, Man, & Salvation*, they stated,

> [John 6] was spoken to the Jews who were rejecting Jesus on the basis of a profession of loyalty to God. Jesus is saying that a true relationship with the Father would inevitably open their eyes to himself. Their rejection of Jesus only demonstrated their alienation from the Father.[13]

Finally, Jerry Walls and Joe Dongell provide additional support for this perspective. They argued the following in their excellent book *Why I Am Not a Calvinist:*

> The Jewish opponents' inability to come to Jesus did not lie, then, in the hidden, eternal plan of God but in their own track record of trampling prior light, of having already denied God himself and spurned God's corrective punishment. Had they received Moses fully, thereby coming to know the Father to the degree possible at that time, they would already have belonged to the Father's flock, and the Father would have drawn them to the Son. But in rejecting Jesus, they demonstrated that they had never surrendered to God in the first place, that they had set their face like flint against all of his continued overtures. Since they did not belong to the Father's own flock, they wouldn't be part of the transfer of sheep already trusting the Father into the fold of the Son. Their spiritual vanity came to full light when they imagined themselves as being qualified to pass judgment on Jesus, the very embodiment of

---

[13] W. T. Purkiser, Richard S. Taylor, and Willard H. Taylor, *God, Man, & Salvation* (Kansas City, MI: Beacon Hill Press, 1977), 430-431.

all truth, while persistently spurning God's lesser lights (e.g., Moses and John the Baptist). Were they willing to drop their pretensions and surrender to God's teaching, they would have been taught by God and led on to the Lord of life.[14]

There is an additional piece of information that needs to be explained in order to grasp the context of John 6. Not only did the Jewish people *not* have a relationship with God, but also, because of their rejection of God's revelation, God was in the process of judging their behavior by hardening their hearts and blinding their eyes. Later in his Gospel, John described this situation in better detail:

> But though he had done so many miracles before them, yet they believed not on him ... *Therefore they could not believe*, because that Esaias said again, He hath blinded their eyes, and hardened their heart; that they should not see with their eyes, nor understand with their heart, and be converted, and I should heal them (John 12:37,39-40).

It is important to emphasize that this judgment did not occur to people who were sincerely seeking the truth and desiring to do God's will. Although there was a remnant, the Jewish people, as a whole, had grown calloused in their rebellious condition, and as a result of this willful stubbornness, God hardened their hearts temporarily to bring about a greater good. William Klein clarifies, "John intends his readers to understand that God's hardening is a response to the adamant self-will of these Jews who reject Christ ...John means not that God prevents the faith of any, but that when people continually reject the truth, God may act to make faith an impossibility by blinding their eyes and hardening their hearts."[15] So, in response to

---

[14] Walls and Dongell, *Why I Am Not a Calvinist*, 75.
[15] William Klein, *The New Chosen People* (Eugene, OR: Wipf & Stock, 2015), 122-123.

the Jews' obstinacy, God prevented them from believing in Christ by sending them a spirit of stupor (Romans 11:8), Jesus' employment of parables (Matthew 13:10-17), and blinding their eyes so that they would not see the truth of Christ (John 12:40).

But, why did God harden their hearts? For what purpose would he prevent a group of people from understanding Christ's person and work? Many Christians might revolt at the suggestion that God acted to ensure that the rebellious Jews would (or could) not believe in Christ. However, the reason for God's judgment was not vindictive, but redemptive. Leighton Flowers explains this beautifully: "It is God's ordained plan to bring redemption to the world through the crucifixion of the Messiah by the hands of the rebellious Jews (Acts 2:23) … They are being temporarily blinded in their already calloused condition so as to accomplish redemption for the world."[16] Thus, God sealed the defiant Jews in their hardened state not because he hated them, but because he desired to bring salvation for the sins of the world through their disobedience.

To understand why God hardened the Jews' hearts to bring about the predestined plan of redemption, an analogy might be helpful. Leighton Flowers offers a useful analogy about a speed trap that captures the intention and purpose of God in sealing the Jewish people in their rebellion. He writes:

> When a police officer sets up a speed trap, he has one ultimate desire: to slow down speeders for the safety of all. However, *by hiding the truth of his presence* he is ensuring that those who want to speed will continue to do so. Thus, in one sense he wants the speeders to continue to speed so as to catch them speeding, but his ultimate purpose is the same: to slow down speeders for the safety of all. The police officer does not determine the speeders' desire to speed in any way, *he simply hides the truth* so as to ensure the speeder will continue to speed, something

---

[16] Flowers, *The Potter's Promise*, 49.

they have freely chosen to do. Never is the will of the
officer in conflict with his good purpose.[17]

During the time of Jesus, the majority of the Jewish people were
not in a faith-relationship with God. Even though they had the
tremendous privilege of possessing the covenants, the law, and the
prophets, they had rejected this revelation of God and were seeking
to establish their own righteousness by works of the law (Romans
9:31,32). Thus, because they did not love God, they did not come
to Christ. As Jesus himself said: "Every man therefore that hath
heard, and hath learned of the Father, cometh unto me" (John 6:45).
Those who had not "learned of the Father" did not come to Christ.
However, God did not waste the stubbornness of these Jewish people;
instead, he used it for a greater good. He solidified them in their
rebellion so that they would crucify Jesus. Just like the police officer
hid his identity from the speeders, Jesus hid his Messianic identity
from the Jewish people so that they would kill him. Had they known
that Jesus was the Messiah, "they would not have crucified the
Lord of glory" (1 Corinthians 2:8). So, by hiding the truth of Jesus's
divine nature and purpose from these disobedient Jewish people
through the use of parabolic language (Mark 4:10-12) and giving
them a spirit of stupor (Romans 11:8), God ensured that salvation
would be provided for the sins of the whole world, according to his
"determinate counsel and foreknowledge" (Acts 2:23).

It is essential to grasp this contextual information before
studying John 6. John 6 was not written in a vacuum, isolated from
time, culture, and people. Without understanding its context, certain
aspects of Calvinism might appear to be plausible. However, this
plausibility disappears once the contextual factors are considered.
Now, before addressing another contextual factor, it might be
helpful to pause and point out how the preceding paragraphs relate
to Calvinism. Again, the aim of this book is to offer a biblical,
theological, and practical critique of Calvinism. In light of God's
hardening the hearts of the Jewish people, one point of contradiction

---

[17] Ibid., 63. Italics mine.

needs to be emphasized in order to further highlight the insufficiency of the Calvinistic system.

The Calvinist perspective on the nature of man is known as total depravity.[18] According to the Calvinistic understanding of total depravity, unregenerate men and women are not able to receive the gospel of Jesus Christ until God raises them to spiritual life. Calvinists David Steele and Curtis Thomas write, "The sinner is so spiritually bankrupt that *he can do nothing pertaining to his salvation* … The natural man is enslaved to sin; he is a child of Satan, rebellious toward God, *blind to truth*, corrupt, and unable to save himself or to prepare himself for salvation."[19] Those who advocate Calvinism do not accept that sinners can believe in the gospel without God's irresistible, supernatural regeneration because they are *blind* to God's truth. All people are born with this spiritual blindness and will never come to God unless he first effectually drags them to himself.

This produces a contradiction, then, for the Calvinist. If all people are spiritually blind from birth, why did God have to blind the Jewish people (John 12:40) to prevent them from seeing the truth of Christ? Wouldn't this be redundant? It would almost be as absurd as placing a blindfold on a blind person. Imagine a father who has a blind son. The father is a godly Christian who sincerely desires to train his young son in the ways of the Lord. As a responsible father, he is aware that many young Christian men have fallen prey to lust and sexual temptation. He obviously does not want this to occur to his son, so he seeks to avoid this tragedy by placing a blindfold on him every time he leaves the house. Whenever someone asks why his son wears a blindfold, he responds, "I want to keep his eyes pure. I don't want him to see anything that would cause him to stumble."

Do you see the absurdity? Everyone with common sense would accuse the father of unnecessary behavior. It is literally impossible

---

[18] More information on total depravity and related topics is in the chapter entitled, "Does Regeneration Precede Faith?"

[19] David N. Steele and Curtis Thomas, *The Five Points of Calvinism* (Phillipsburg, NJ: Presbyterian & Reformed Publishing Co., 1963), 25. Italics his.

for his son to see anything, including lewd images that could lead to sexual immorality. Placing the blindfold on the blind son accomplishes nothing, except exposing the lunacy of the father. Likewise, if it is true that all people are born without the capacity to receive Christ apart from God's act of regeneration, then it is also unnecessary for God to give people "eyes that they should not see, and ears that they should not hear" (Romans 11:8). All unregenerate people, according to Calvinism, cannot possibly see God's truth, so blinding people who are already blind portrays God as insecure and afraid that someone will believe the truth who isn't supposed to. In other words, if Calvinism is true, God is blinding the eyes of spiritually blind people, even though they already cannot see the truth of Jesus Christ. Why God would conduct himself in this demented fashion is a conundrum that only makes sense in the minds of those whose twisted theology demands it.

So far, we have focused on one group of Jewish people in our study of the background to John 6. The context is incomplete, however, since not every Jewish person had rejected the light of God's revelation. There was a group of Jewish people who were sincerely seeking God. Paul Marston and Roger Forster state that this group of sincere Israelites "contained those who had received John's baptism of repentance, and in faith-relationship were waiting for God to reveal his coming kingdom."[20] This host of "true and genuine Jewish believers in God" consisted of several individuals who are named in the New Testament: "Zechariah, Elizabeth, John the Baptist, Anna, Simeon, the disciples, and so."[21] These were true obedient followers of God who had been not only taught by God but listened to and learned from him (John 6:45).

Furthermore, because these individuals were in a right relationship with the Father, they were given to Christ and drawn to him. Thus, the people given to Jesus Christ (John 6:37,39) were

---

[20] Paul Marston and Roger Forster, *God's Strategy in Human History* (Eugene, OR: Wipf & Stock, 2000), 278.

[21] John Lennox, *Determined to Believe?* (Grand Rapids, MI: Zondervan, 2017), 174.

men and women who had already received the revelation from God through Moses and the prophets. Jesus expressed this clearly: "I have manifested thy name unto the men which thou gavest me out of the world: *thine they were*, and thou gavest them me; and they have kept thy word" (John 17:6). Notice the italicized portion of this verse. The individuals given to Jesus were the Father's people. As Marshall writes, "The men whom the Father gives to Jesus are those Jews who have already responded to Him."[22] They were "of God" in the sense that they had a relationship with him, and God gave them to Jesus while he was "down from heaven."

These faithful Jewish believers, who had "learned of the Father" (John 6:45), were given to Christ, would be drawn to him, and would consequently come to believe in him throughout Jesus's earthly ministry (John 6:37). Marston and Forster provide an excellent summary of the background to the Jewish peoples' coming to believe in Jesus Christ:

> Only those in Israel who are spiritually discerning and in relationship with the Father are able to understand what Jesus is teaching … All the Jews were given God's teaching, but only those who listened to God and learned from him would be drawn to Jesus … If anyone really wanted to do the will of God, then God would show him what the teaching meant (John 7:17). Those Jews who are really seeking God's will for their lives, ongoing in a faith-relationship with him, will be drawn by God to come to Christ.[23]

A classic example of this "coming historically to believe in Jesus as the Son of God"[24] is Simeon in Luke 2:

---

[22] Marshall, *Kept by the Power of God*, 180.

[23] Marston and Forster, *God's Strategy in Human History*, 278-280.

[24] Lennox, *Determined to Believe?*, 174.

> There was a man in Jerusalem, whose name was
> Simeon; and the same man was just and devout,
> waiting for the consolation of Israel: and the Holy
> Ghost was upon him. And it was revealed unto him
> by the Holy Ghost, that he should not see death,
> before he had seen the Lord's Christ. And he came
> by the Spirit into the temple: and when the parents
> brought in the child Jesus, to do for him after the
> custom of the law, then took he him up in his arms,
> and blessed God, and said, Lord, now lettest thou
> thy servant depart in peace, according to thy word:
> for mine eyes have seen thy salvation, which thou
> hast prepared before the fact of all people; a light
> to lighten the Gentiles, and the glory of thy people
> Israel … (Luke 2:25-32).

Simeon is surely a man who had listened to and learned from the Father. Because he knew God, he was drawn by the Father to Jesus and understood that he was the Messiah. This beautifully illustrates the meaning of John 6:45, which records the words of Christ: "Every man therefore that hath heard, and hath learned of the Father, cometh unto me." Only those Jews, like Simeon, who had welcomed the revelation of the Father would come to Jesus. Marshall concludes, "For a Jew to come to Jesus is possible only if he is 'open' to the revelation of the Father which he has already received."[25]

Now, this contextual information is either omitted or ignored by Calvinists in their prejudiced interpretation of John 6. Not equipped with a proper understanding of the background to Jesus's teaching in John 6, many vulnerable Christians have been led astray into accepting the damnable doctrines of unconditional election, irresistible grace, and the inevitable perseverance of believers. However, once the context is grasped, the use of this wonderful chapter to support the theological system of Calvinism is found to be improper and an appalling illustration of blatant eisegesis.

---

[25] Marshall, *Kept by the Power of God*, 180.

Wrenching verses from their surrounding context is a tool employed by false teachers to establish their erroneous doctrines, but it should be avoided passionately by those who are interested in "rightly dividing the word of truth" (2 Timothy 2:15).

A Deeper Look at a Few Verses in John 6

As noted previously, John 6 has suffered extreme abuse at the hands of Calvinists who are seeking to locate support for their theological system. The following four verses appear repeatedly throughout Calvinistic literature:

John 6:37- All that the Father giveth me shall come to me; and him that cometh to me I will in no wise cast out.

John 6:39- And this is the Father's will which hath sent me, that of all which he hath given me I should lose nothing, but should raise it up again at the last day.

John 6:44- No man can come to me, except the Father which hath sent me draw him: and I will raise him up at the last day.

John 6:65- And he said, Therefore said I unto you, that no man can come unto me, except it were given unto him of my Father.

Because of the frequency with which these verses are quoted in support of Calvinism, it is necessary to investigate each of these verses. If you want to intellectually engage Calvinists in the hopes of refuting their position, you must make an effort to understand what their interpretation of these verses is and why their interpretation is faulty and unbiblical. Honestly, the consistency with which

Calvinists employ the same arguments is both frightening and astounding. Calvinists in every geographical location will use the exact same proof-texts to defend their theology. You can be sure that if you get into a debate with a Calvinist, he will quickly cite different verses in John 6 to defend his perspective. Possessing sound objections to his biased eisegesis might force him to reevaluate his doctrinal stance.

Again, John 6:37 is often cited by Calvinists to uphold different elements of their theological system. What this verse means to a Calvinist is this: God has given a certain group of people to Jesus Christ, known as the elect, who will necessarily come to believe in Jesus at God's appointed time. In other words, the expression "all that the Father giveth me" refers to those that he has unconditionally chosen for salvation in eternity past. John Calvin insisted that God "determined with himself whatever he wished to happen with regard to every man. All are not created on equal terms, but some are preordained to eternal life, others to eternal damnation; and, accordingly, as each has been created for one or other of these ends, we say that he has been predestinated to life or to death."[26] Those who are "preordained to eternal life" are the ones that the Father gives to Jesus, and they will come to Jesus at the designated hour. Apparently, that's why Jesus is so optimistic. He knows that the elect will inevitably believe in him. As Calvinist theologian D. A Carson stated, "Jesus' confidence in the success of his mission is frankly predestinarian."[27] Further, once the elect come to Jesus, they are eternally secure. Christ "will in no wise cast [them] out."

Initially, the Calvinistic explanation of John 6:37 makes sense. This understanding, however, is driven by *a priori* assumption read into the passage and fails to take into consideration the context of what is happening during Jesus's earthly ministry. One thing to emphasize is the corporate aspect to Jesus's statement. The phrase

---

[26] Calvin, *Institutes of the Christian Religion*, 610.

[27] D. A. Carson, *The Pillar New Testament Commentary- The Gospel According to John* (Grand Rapids, MI: William B. Eerdmans Company, 1991). Accessed with Logos Bible Software.

"all that" is a "collective use of the neuter singular."[28] According to Ben Witherington III, this "suggests the verse is referring to an elect group, not elect individuals."[29] Even Carson, an influential Calvinist, admits that "all that" is "a singular neuter ... used to refer to the elect collectively,"[30] although he inserts the notion of unconditional election into his interpretation, something completely unwarranted by the biblical text. Jesus affirms, then, in the first clause of John 6:37 that the ones given to him, as a group, would come to him. Furthermore, in the second clause, he emphasizes that he would not reject anyone who came to him in faith for eternal life.

John 6:37 does not refer to God's action of giving some people to Christ in eternity past who will come to him. James White is an example of a Calvinist who finds an eternal decree in this verse. He writes, "The giving of the Father inevitably results in the coming of the believer, not the other way around. The *divine decree* of the Father in giving a people to Christ is the grounds of our coming to Christ."[31] This idea of pre-temporal election is not found in John 6, so those who argue for unconditional election and irresistible grace based on the Father's giving some to Jesus do so because of theological presuppositions, not because of honest exegesis. Importantly, according to John 6:37, when does this giving occur? David Allen explains, "Not in eternity past, for the use of the present-tense verb indicates contemporary action: the Father was in the very process of giving to the Son those who were believing on him."[32]

Who, then, are the ones that the Father is giving to Jesus Christ? As noted previously, the Father is giving Jesus the faithful Jewish

[28] A.T. Robertson, *Word Pictures in the New Testament*- Vol. IV (Nashville, TN: Broadman Press, 1931), 107.

[29] Ben Witherington III, *John's Wisdom* (Louisville, KY: Westminster John Knox Press, 1995), 158.

[30] Carson, *Gospel According to John*. Accessed with Logos Bible Software.

[31] Accessed at http://www.aomin.org/aoblog/1998/12/05/the-believers-security-a-response-to-james-akin/. Italics mine.

[32] David L. Allen, *The Extent of the Atonement* (Nashville, TN: B&H Academic, 2016), 697.

remnant. Jesus suggested this: "I have manifested thy name unto the men which thou gavest me out of the world: *thine they were*, and thou gavest them me; and they have kept thy word" (John 17:6). These belonged to the Father's flock and were given to Jesus Christ. John 6:37 indicates that this transfer of sheep from the Father to the Son had already begun. Those given to Jesus would trust in him for eternal life, and he would "in no wise" refuse anyone who came to him.

Calvinists use essentially the same arguments from John 6:39 as they do from John 6:37. However, they often emphasize the fact that Jesus says that it is the Father's will that he should lose none of those given to him. Then, the Calvinist will ask: Is it possible for Jesus to fail to accomplish the Father's will? Several points can be made in response to this objection.

For starters, we must not forget that God's will, according to the Scriptures, is not always brought to pass. While God has a cosmic plan that cannot be thwarted, individuals can reject God's plan for their lives. Marston and Forster note, "Human beings, of course, could not thwart God's ultimate plan for the world, but they both can and do thwart his plan that they, as individuals, should have a part in it."[33] Marston and Forster's contention is well-established in the Bible. God wants everyone to be saved, even though everyone will not be saved (1 Timothy 2:4). The will of God for believers is that they abstain from sexual immorality, yet many Christians fall prey to sexual temptation (1 Thessalonians 4:3). In all things, the body of Christ is to give thanks (1 Thessalonians 5:18). However, many members of the church grumble and complain about the circumstances of life instead of rejoicing about what they have in Jesus. Similarly, just because it was God's will for Jesus to lose none of those given to him does not necessarily mean that it was impossible for him to lose any. God's will for individuals is not always accomplished (Luke 7:30).

As a matter of fact, the Scriptures indicate that Jesus did lose someone given to him, not because of any impotency on Christ's

---

[33] Marston and Forster, *God's Strategy in Human History*, 110.

part, but because God has created human beings as volitional creatures with the power of choice. In Jesus's lengthy prayer in John 17, he reveals: "While I was with them in the world, I kept them in thy name: *those that thou gavest me I have kept, and none of them is lost, but the son of perdition*; that the scripture might be fulfilled" (John 17:12). Was Judas given to Jesus? Yes. This demonstrates that being given to Christ did not eliminate the possibility of apostasy. Jesus faithfully kept everyone who remained in his firm grasp. Robert Shank's observation is fitting:

> Certainly there is nothing ineffectual about the keeping grace of the Father; it is infinite. But neither was there anything lacking in the keeping power of Jesus ... Those whom the Father gave Him Jesus kept- except one. Neither the Father nor the Son can keep those who do not wish to accept the conditions under which they may be kept. It is not, as some foolishly assert, a question of whether men are "stronger than God." Nor is it a question of what God *could* do. It is only a question of what God does do, as revealed in the Holy Scriptures. The Scriptures declare that men are free to depart from God, and believers are solemnly warned against so doing (Hebrews 3:12).[34]

Both John 6:44 and John 6:65 suffer the same type of contextual abuse from the Calvinist. Again, Jesus said: " No man can come to me, except the Father which hath sent me draw him" (6:44) and "no man can come unto me, except it were given unto him of my Father" (6:65). We will look to the interpretation of R. C. Sproul to get an idea of how Calvinists view these passages. Sproul's comments are typical of what a person will likely hear from an advocate of Calvinism about John 6. After quoting John 6:65, he writes:

---

[34] Robert Shank, *Life in the Son* (Springfield, MI: Westcott House, 1961), 277.

The first element of this teaching is a *universal negative*. The words "no one" are all-inclusive.[35] They allow for no exception apart from the exceptions Jesus adds. The next word is crucial. It is the word *can*. This has to do with ability, not permission … In this passage Jesus is not saying, "No one is allowed to come to me …" He is saying, "No one is *able* to come to me …" … The next word in the passage is also vital. "Unless" refers to what we call a *necessary condition*. A necessary condition refers to something that must happen before something else can happen. The meaning of Jesus' words is clear. No human being can possibly come to Christ unless something happens that makes it possible for him to come. That necessary condition Jesus declares is that "it has been granted to him by the Father." Jesus is saying here that the ability to come to him is a gift from God. Man does not have the ability in and of himself to come to Christ. God must do something first.[36]

This is representative of Calvinistic interpretation on John 6:44 and John 6:65. According to Calvinism, all human beings are born without the capacity to come to God apart from his effectual

---

[35] It would be interesting to know how exactly Sproul knew that these words were intended to refer to all men without exception, while the passages that speak of Christ's dying for all men (1 Timothy 2:6) are to be interpreted in a limited fashion. Later, in this same book, Sproul writes, "Wherever it is said that Christ died for all, *some limitation must be added* or the conclusion would have to be universalism or a mere potential atonement" (*Chosen by God*, 207, italics mine). Sproul reveals his bias when he says that "some limitation must be added." The only necessity for the limitation is his theology, not the Scriptures. Furthermore, Sproul has failed to distinguish between the provision of the atonement and its application. The atonement is sufficient for the whole world but efficient only for those who believe.

[36] Sproul, *Chosen by God*, 67-68.

work of grace. No one is able to believe the gospel without divine enablement, and this divine enablement is always efficacious. Thus, those who reject the gospel have not been drawn by the Father (or it had not been given to them). The ability to receive Christ as Lord and Savior is a gift from God given only to the elect.

This explanation fails to account fully for the biblical witness. First, according to the Calvinist, the drawing of the Father in John 6:44 is irresistible; those who are drawn will necessarily come to Christ. This argument crumbles in light of the fact that the same word for draw is used in John 12:32, where Jesus declares, "And I, if I be lifted up from the earth, will *draw* all men unto me." Roger Olson concludes, "If the Greek word for 'draw' in John 6:44 can only mean 'drag' or 'compel' rather than 'woo' or 'call,' then John 12:32 must be interpreted as teaching universal salvation."[37] Those who embrace Reformed theology generally are aware of this conundrum and respond in a manner similar to D. A. Carson:

> Many attempt to dilute the force of the claim by referring to 12:32, where the same verb for 'to draw' (*helkyō*) occurs: Jesus there claims he will draw 'all men' to himself. The context shows rather clearly, however, that 12:32 refers to 'all men without distinction' (*i.e.* not just Jews) rather than to 'all men without exception'.[38]

In other words, to the Calvinist, the "no man" in John 6:44 refers to all men without exception, while the "all men" in John 12:32 includes only some men. It is arbitrary to assign a universal scope to "no man" in John 6:44 and 6:65 but a limitation to "all men" in John 12:32. Shank's reflection is so true: "Men who approach the Bible with the presuppositions of Calvinism invariably become entangled in confusion and absurd contradictions which are an offense both

---

[37] Roger Olson, *Against Calvinism* (Grand Rapids, MI: Zondervan, 2011), 51.
[38] Carson, *Gospel According to John*. Accessed with Logos Bible Software.

to common sense and (what is worse) to the testimony of the Holy Scriptures."[39]

Furthermore, the Calvinistic interpretation does not consider the context of John 6. Once more, Sproul, who is representative of the Reformed approach, discusses these passages without even attempting to supply the basic background information. Here are the surrounding verses of John 6:44:

> The Jews then murmured at him, because he said, I am the bread which came down from heaven. And they said, Is not this Jesus, the son of Joseph, whose father and mother we know? How is it then that he saith, I came down from heaven? Jesus therefore answered and said unto them, Murmur not among yourselves. No man can come to me, except the Father which hath sent me draw him: and I will raise him up at the last day. It is written in the prophets, And they shall be all taught of God. Every man therefore that hath heard, and hath learned of the Father, cometh unto me (John 6:41-45).

Jesus is in discussion with "the Jews" (v. 41). Particularly, these are Jewish people who have a false idea of the Messiah and, as previously mentioned, are not in a relationship with God. They begin to murmur amongst themselves because Jesus had just declared: "I am the bread of life" and "I came down from heaven." How could these things be true? After all, they knew Jesus's parents, so it must have been impossible for him to have literally descended from heaven. This confusion about the Messiah's teaching further strengthens the case that the majority of the Jews did not truly desire to do the Father's will. This is evident in John 7:16,17: "Jesus answered them [the Jews], and said, My doctrine is not mine, but his that sent me. If any man will do his will, he shall know of the doctrine, whether it be of God, or whether I speak of myself." The Jews did not want to do

---

[39] Shank, *Life in the Son*, 178.

God's will and were thus incapable of perceiving the spiritual origin of Jesus and his words. Had these men and women been of God, they would have heard God's words through the lips of Jesus (John 8:47).

Jesus responded to the complaints of the Jews by instructing them not to "murmur ... among yourselves. No man can come to me, except the Father which hath sent me draw him ... Every man therefore that hath heard, and hath learned of the Father cometh unto me." What is Jesus saying, in context? Walls and Dongell answer this well, "Jesus was addressing hostile Jewish leaders who were in fact rejecting the teaching of Jesus. We must conclude, then, that Jesus claim (that the Father *must* draw any who would come to Jesus) stands as the precise explanation for why these very hearers had rejected Jesus: the Father had not drawn them!"[40]

However, the reason why the Father did not draw these Jewish opponents to Jesus is not because of some mysterious decree of God that assigned some to eternal salvation and others to eternal perdition, but because the Jewish leaders had not truly listened to the Father. Only those Jewish believers who had listened to the Father were drawn by the Father to Jesus. Marston and Forster are correct: "Only those in Israel who are spiritually discerning and in relationship with the Father are able to understand what Jesus is teaching."[41] As Jesus emphatically said, "Every man therefore that hath heard, and hath learned of the Father, cometh unto me" (John 6:45). Many of the Jews did not come to Jesus because they were not drawn by the Father to Jesus, and the reason why they were not drawn to Jesus is because they had not accepted "the revelation of God which He had already given before the coming of Jesus."[42] It was, therefore, foolish for the Jewish people to complain about Jesus Christ, since their refusal "to come to Christ was due to their refusal to listen to the Father."[43]

---

[40] Walls and Dongell, *Why I Am Not a Calvinist*, 74.

[41] Marston and Forster, *God's Strategy for Human History*, 278.

[42] Marshall, *Kept by the Power of God*, 179.

[43] Allen, *The Extent of the Atonement*, 697.

Chapter 2

Election and Ephesians 1

One of the proof-texts used by Calvinists to support the erroneous doctrine of unconditional election is Ephesians 1:1-14. Briefly stated, unconditional election advocates that God, before the foundation of the world, chose a section of mankind to be saved (the elect), and the remainder of mankind (the non-elect) to be eternally damned. To refute this doctrine and properly explain the meaning of Ephesians 1:1-14, the following steps will be followed. First, a vertical and horizontal reading of the text will be presented. Second, a brief analysis of Old Testament and first-century thinking will be addressed. Third, proper exegesis of the text will be offered. Fourth, noted scholars and theologians will be referenced to support the contention that corporate election is the proper interpretation of Ephesians 1:1-14.

Vertical and Horizontal Reading

The first issue to address is the phrase "chosen us in him before the foundation of the world" (Ephesians 1:4). It should be noted that in the book of Ephesians there are over 150 plural personal pronouns and antecedents, and other plural words, used to reference the "saints" and "faithful in Christ Jesus" in Ephesians 1:1. In addition, there are over forty references to Jesus Christ, such as "in Christ" and "in him," in the book of Ephesians. In the first chapter, there are at least fifteen personal references to being "in Christ" and giving "praise of the glory of *his* grace" and enjoying the blessings of Christ. One may observe in a quick reading of the book of Ephesians a glimpse of two important factors that Paul is going to address. First, the abundance of the usage of plural words points to the idea that Paul is thinking not about individualistic election, but about the corporate election of the church. Second, the abundance of references to Jesus Christ makes Him the focus, and the blessings He has predestined for the redeemed are found *only* in Him. Thus, the first step of observation concerning the rich blessings of Christ listed in Ephesians 1 reveals a foundational aspect of Pauline theology: election is both corporate and Christocentric.

The question must be asked concerning Paul's usage of the pronoun "us." Is Paul's focus on individuals or the collective body of the church? Clearly, the focus of Paul's writing is the church, as Hofmann observes, "The body of Christians is the object of this choice, not as composed of a certain number of individuals-a sum of 'the elect' opposed to a sum of the non-elect-but as the Church taken out of and separated from the world."[44] Lightfoot noted that "the election to salvation is only in union with Christ. Thus, Christ is the *locus standi* of election, apart from whom no man is elect ... the election of Christ involves implicitly the election of the Church."[45] Thus, "us" in Ephesians 1:4 should be interpreted in its larger meaning to represent the church and not be interpreted to imply personal individualistic election. Clearly, as Shank insightfully comments, "the corporate body of the elect is comprised of individuals. But the election is primarily corporate and only secondarily particular. The thesis that the election is corporate, as Paul understood it and viewed it in the Ephesian doxology, is supported by the whole context

---

[44] W. Robertson Nicoll, *The Expositor's Bible: The Epistle to the Ephesians* (New York, NY: George H. Doran Company, n. d.), 31.
[45] Qtd in Shank, *Elect in the Son*, 44-45.

of his epistle."[46] The observation of noted preacher and pastor Harold J. Ockenga is consistent with the thesis that Paul's meaning in Ephesians 1:4 is in reference to the corporate election of the church: "Those who are 'in Christ' are the Church, and it was this Church which God chose before the foundation of the world to share His gift and to become the bride of Christ."[47]

Finally, it needs to be reiterated that the focus of Ephesians 1:4 is on Christ ("in him") who is the Predestinated One (Isaiah 42:1; 1 Peter 2:6) and what God has predestinated in Him. Charles Ellicott reasoned, "The whole reference is to the election 'in Christ' by the foreknowledge of God, of those who should hereafter be made His members ... It will be observed that even here it clearly refers to all members of the Church, without distinction."[48] Distinguished theologian C. I. Scofield noted in his Reference Bible that the election, 'chosen us,' addressed in Ephesians 1:4, is corporate as to the church. A careful reading of Ephesians 1, followed by the vertical and horizontal reading of the specific text of Ephesians 1:1-14, leads us to the conclusion that election is Christocentric and corporate. Therefore, we may correctly conclude that "Ephesians chapter one is not about God predetermining which individuals will be in Christ. This passage is about God predetermining the spiritual blessings for those who are in Christ through believing the word of truth."[49]

Old Testament and First-Century Thinking

It is important to note that cultural and historical contexts, geography, and Bible manners and customs are just a few factors to consider when properly interpreting Scriptures. Thus, to obtain a

---

[46] Ibid., 45.

[47] Harold J. Ockenga, *Faithful in Christ Jesus* (New York: NY: Fleming H. Revell Company, 1948), 32.

[48] Charles J. Ellicott, *Ellicott's Commentary on the Whole Bible – Vol. 7-8* (Grand Rapids, MI: Zondervan Publishing House, 1959), 16.

[49] Flowers, *The Potter's Promise*, 79.

proper understanding of Ephesians 1:1-14, a study of the historical-grammatical context of this text will provide valuable insight into Apostle Paul's original intent. However, before beginning that study an investigation and evaluation of election in the Old Testament will prove to be very useful. For starters, the Hebrew word *bachra*, which means to "choose," is applicable both to individuals who are called for specific purposes of service and to the corporate nation of Israel. Thus, it should be noted that "in no way can this imply that God chose all or even specific individual Israelites for eternal salvation."[50] In addition, the Hebrew word *bahir*, which means elect, is predominately used in the plural tense. Consequently, "election terminology affirms the astounding conviction that the eternal God has chosen a people, Israel ... Divine election in its basic Old Testament form is collective, corporate, national. It encompasses a community of which the individual Israelite is an integral part."[51] Theologian Brian J. Abasciano contends that the concept of election in the Old Testament is clearly corporate. He argues that "the locus of election was the covenant community and that individuals found their election through membership in the elect people."[52]

The second source to consider in Old Testament and first-century thinking is the extra-biblical literature written from 300 B.C. to A.D. 70. Prominent theologian William W. Klein presents a careful evaluation of the Apocryphal and Pseudepigrapha. His conclusions are insightful:

1. God chooses certain things and places for His purposes.
2. Individuals are chosen by God for specific ministries.
3. However, election terminology generally references the corporate body of Israel.

---

[50] Klein, *The New Chosen People*, 8.

[51] Ibid., 11-12.

[52] Brian J. Abasciano, "Corporate Election in Romans 9," *JETS* 49 (2006): 353.

Klein continues, "Though the nation as a whole may be elect in one important sense, not all individual Israelites are 'elect unto salvation' or elect in the eternal and salvific sense."[53] In addition, he notes that "in no cases do we find reference to God's choice of individuals as an election to their individual salvation."[54] An additional observation from Klein's influential work will strengthen the corporate view of election. In his evaluation of the Dead Sea Scrolls, he reached the conclusion that "this corporate self-consciousness seems to be even more pronounced than that expressed in the Old Testament for the entire nation."[55] Finally, a brief examination of the rabbinical writings also yielded the conclusion that election was corporate, but Israelites had the capacity and responsibility to join this corporate body.

The third point to consider in seeking to understand the context of Ephesians 1:1-14 is the first-century thinking of Judaism. Distinguished professor Brian Abasciano provides greater support of the corporate view of election. His findings on first-century thinking of Judaism are quite compelling. He noted, "The Mediterranean Hellenistic culture of the first-century was collectivist rather than individualistic in outlook, and first-century Judaism was even more so. This means … that the dominate perspective of Paul and his contemporaries was that the group was primary and the individual secondary."[56] To further substantiate his findings, Abasciano cites author and professor Gary Burnett, who observed "that Paul's culture was collective rather than individualistic in orientation and that there was little individualism in the first-century."[57] A study of Old Testament theology, and in particular the context of the definitions of Hebrew words, leads to a corporate view of election. As a matter of fact, according to Abasciano, "The corporate nature of the election of God's people in the Old Testament is so well recognized that Moo,

---

[53] Klein, *The New Chosen People*, 24.

[54] Ibid., 25.

[55] Ibid., 34.

[56] Abasciano, "Corporate Election in Romans 9," 356.

[57] Ibid., 357.

an advocate of individual election in Paul's thought and Romans 9, concedes that Paul would have found only corporate election in the Scriptures and his Jewish tradition."[58] Finally, the social and historical-grammatical contextualization of Paul's writing presents a strong argument for his view that election was corporate. We conclude that when it comes to election unto salvation Paul uses not individualistic but corporate language.

Exegesis of the Text – Ephesians 1:1-14

Before beginning this section, a comment about foreknowledge is warranted. This will establish the platform for a proper hermeneutical approach to this important passage of Scripture. Ellicott observes, "Foreknowledge does not interfere with free will because the foreknowledge, though prior in point of time, is posterior in the order of causation to the act of choice."[59] Since God is before time, and created time, He is not subject to time. Thus, the eternality of God allows Him to always act in the present. Because of God's eternality and immutability, He possesses eternal and unchanging knowledge. It follows then that God is omniscient and knows all choices that will ever be made, but He does not predetermine or foreordain them. It should be noted that salvific responses to the gospel message of redemption are by faith in the word of truth as revealed in Ephesians 1:13. This clearly indicates that there is synergistic activity and the interaction of the divine influence of the Holy Spirit and man's free will are engaged in the process of man deciding to accept or reject God's gracious invitation of salvation. As Geisler explains, "If salvation comes by faith-which Scripture plainly affirms (Ephesians 2:8-9)-then faith is logically prior to being regenerated ... We do not get saved in order to believe; rather, we believe in order to become saved."[60]

---

[58] Ibid., 353.

[59] Ellicott, *Commentary on the Whole Bible*, 238.

[60] Norman L. Geisler, *Systematic Theology in One Volume* (Minneapolis, MN: Bethany House, 2011), 822.

It must be emphatically stated that the doctrine of unconditional election errors in advocating that God indelibly established before the foundation of the world who would be eternally saved (elect) and who would be eternally damned (non-elect). In addition, Reformed theology errors in its monergistic approach to salvation. The New Testament books of Hebrews and Galatians declare that those who have come out of the bondage of sin into the liberty of salvation may return to such bondage. Foreknowledge does not negate freedom. Renowned theologian Dale Moody posited, "It is not predetermined that foreknowledge will always be followed by predestination, calling, justification and glorification as were the words at the end of Romans 8. That is the normal sequence, but the sequence can be broken at any point by turning again to slavery."[61] Finally, historical Christianity unreservedly supports the argument against the election and predestination of individuals to salvation or damnation. Frank Stagg states very soberly, "One is strangely insensitive to the throb and pulse of the whole New Testament if he thinks that each man's fate is determined for him in advance."[62]

With a thorough vertical and horizontal reading of Ephesians 1:1-14, and a profitable investigation and evaluation of Old Testament theology and first-century Jewish thinking, a foundation has been laid and a pathway established to move forward in a proper biblical exegesis of this important text. In addition, the social and historical-grammatical contextualization of Paul's writing, as will be demonstrated, presents a strong argument that election is Christocentric and corporate.

Before focusing on the Christocentricity of election, definitions need to be offered. Election and elect come from the Greek words *eklekos* and *ekloge,* which mean picked out, selected, chosen, and a picking out or selection. Thus, election is God's act of choosing. In addition, the word predestinate comes from the Greek word

---

[61] Dale Moody, *The Word of Truth* (Grand Rapids, MI: Wm. B. Eerdmans Publishing House, 1981), 343-44.

[62] Frank Stagg, *New Testament Theology* (Nashville, TN: Broadman Press, 1962), 88.

*proorizo,*which means to limit in advance or determine beforehand. It is important to understand how these definitions are applicable to the scriptural text of Ephesians 1:3-5. In addition, what and when did God predestinate? One must first understand election and predestination appropriately as it is affixed to Christ. Attention must be given to the predestination of Christ. Though pretemporal in design and declaration, it is historical through the death and resurrection of Jesus Christ. Christ is the Elect and Chosen One (Isaiah 42:1-8) and John declares him to be the "Lamb slain from the foundation of the world" (Revelation 13:8). At the cross one sees the manifestation of God's sovereign will interacting with man's free will and responsibility. Jesus Christ is the focus of time and eternity, and Paul had that thought in mind when he wrote: "But we speak the wisdom of God in a mystery, even the hidden wisdom, which God ordained before the world unto our glory" (1 Corinthians 2:7).

The first major point to emphasize and examine is that election is Christocentric. To simplify the understanding of this truth, one must consider the predestination *of* Christ. From the protoevangelium of Genesis 3:15, to the Paschal Lamb of Egypt, to the Lamb of God in the Garden of Gethsemane, the unfolding drama of redemption is being fulfilled. From the founding of the New Testament church in Acts 2, through the eschatological pages of the Book of Revelation, the message is clear. The repeated revelation is the predestination *of* Christ and the predestination *in* Christ. This truth is the foundational principle that allows the composite understanding of all history. Finally, in reference to Jesus, Luke 24:37 states, "And beginning at Moses and all the prophets, he expounded unto them in all the scriptures the things concerning himself." Through the timeframe of the first patriarchs into the typology of the Old Testament sacrifices and Levitical priesthood God's plan of redemption slowly unfolds. From the prophetic voices of the Old Testament prophets and across dispensational boundaries the progressive revelation emerges that the eternal Son of God will become flesh and be the sacrifice for the sin of the world. John writes of the embodiment of many of the Old Testament types, shadows, and prophecies in the divine incarnation in John 1:1-14. In addition, the truth of the necessity of Christ's death and resurrection is revealed in Acts 2:23-24 which states, "Him, being delivered by the determinate counsel and foreknowledge of God, ye have taken, and by wicked hands have crucified and slain; Whom God hath raised up, having loosed the pains of death; because it was not possible that he should be holden of it." Thus, the election and predestination of Jesus Christ as the Savior of the world reveals that salvation was not an afterthought of God.

A second factor to consider in understanding that election is Christocentric is that predestination is *in* Christ. One notices when reading Ephesians 1 the repeated emphasis on phrases such as "in him" and "in Christ" and "in the beloved." Clearly, Paul is focused on the phrase "in him" in v.4, and not on the phrase "chosen us" or individualistic salvation. Corey Newman remarked, "Election is profoundly Christological. Paul's 'in Christ' language legitimately bears an enormous amount of interpretive weight; here the small prepositional phrase 'in him' (*en auto*) points to the way God fulfills his purposes."[63] Paul begins to expound upon his reference to all spiritual blessings in Christ (1:3) by establishing the qualifier "in him." This supports Abasciano's contention that "it is because of Christ's election that incorporation into him entails the extension of his election to those who are so united to him."[64] He offered additional insight into Ephesians 1:4 by stating that "the election of human beings is directly qualified in the verse by the phrase "in him" which indicates the sphere and manner of the election of the human beings mentioned – which contradicts unconditional individualistic election."[65] Thus, God chose the church as a result of man's incorporation in Christ. Noted biblical author Theodore Epp wrote in support of the predestination of Christ and opposed the

---

[63] Corey C. Newman, "Election and Predestination in Ephesians 1:4-6a: An Exegetical-Theological Study of the Historical, Christological Realization of God's Purpose," *Review and Expositor* 93 (1996): 238.

[64] Brian J. Abasciano, "Clearing up Misconceptions about Corporate Election," *Ashland Theological Journal* 41, (2009): 71.

[65] Ibid., 72.

teaching of the predestination of the 'elect' and the 'non-elect.' He stated concerning Ephesians 1:4, "The choice involved is not God's choosing some for salvation and some for condemnation but his choosing certain things for the one who already has received Jesus Christ as Saviour."[66]

To further support the argument that election is Christocentric and predestination is in Christ, William Klein contends:

> The preposition 'in' may have an instrumental sense-
> the blessings come through Christ. However, the
> locative sense of inclusion in Christ is the dominant
> sense ... Believers experience the blessings of the
> heavenly realms not only through Christ's agency
> but also because they are incorporated into the
> exalted Christ as their representative, who is himself
> in the heavenly realms.[67]

An additional comment by Dale Moody further strengthens the idea that Paul's focus in Ephesians 1:4 is on 'in him' and not on 'chosen us.' Concerning Paul (Ephesians 1:4) and Peter (1 Peter 2:8), he writes, "Neither of the two great Apostles teaches the absolute and deterministic predestination developed in the tradition of Augustine and Calvin ... Both Paul and Peter teach that there is a human condition attached to predestination, and that condition is the free response of faith."[68]

The second major point to emphasize and examine is that election is corporate. It is important to start this discussion by analyzing the word "us" in Ephesians 1:4. Carey Newman observes, "God chose 'us' (*hemas*), a people. *Hemas*, a first person, plural, personal pronoun, falls within 'the language of belonging' and

---

[66] Theodore H. Epp, *Living Abundantly* (Lincoln, NE: Back to the Bible, 1973), 40.
[67] Temper Longman III and David E. Garland, *The Expositor's Bible Commentary-Volume 12* (Grand Rapids, MI: Zondervan, 2006), 48.
[68] Moody, *The Word of Truth*, 347.

refers to the Christian Church, to those who are in Christ."[69] In addition, this observation is corroborated by the following reference from Lange's Commentary: "us – the reference is not to individuals in themselves, to the sum of individuals at that time, but to the Church and its growth externally and internally, yet in such a way that each individual may refer it to himself."[70] A careful study of Pauline theology does not diminish the personal aspect of election. However, in this text Paul does not "assert here particular or individual election, i.e., that God has selected specific individuals for inclusion in the church. He underscores the church's election in Christ, who is God's elect one (Lk 9:35; 23:35). Being incorporated in Christ, the church attains its identity, all of its blessings, and its chosen position."[71] A consideration of the predestination of Christ and the predestination in Christ, as well as a proper exegesis of the text under consideration, yields the insightful conclusion that election is Christocentric and corporate. Influential writer Robert Shank very powerfully and succinctly summarizes this position: "Election and predestination, coextensive, are corporate and comprehend individuals only in association and identification with the elect body. Election and predestination comprehend all men potentially, no man unconditionally, and the Israel of God efficiently."[72] Ben Witherington III concurs:

> The concept of election and destining here is a corporate one. If one is in him, one is elect and destined. Paul is not talking about pretemporal electing or choosing of individual humans outside of Christ to be in Christ, but rather of the election

---

[69] Newman, "Election and Predestination in Ephesians 1:4-6a: An Exegetical-Theological
Study of the Historical, Christological Realization of God's Purpose," 239.
[70] John Peter Lange, *Commentary on the Holy Scriptures: Galatians-Colossians* (Grand Rapids, MI: Zondervan Publishing House, n.d.), 80.
[71] Longman III and Garland, *Expositor's Bible Commentary*, 48-49.
[72] Shank, *Elect in the Son*, 157.

of Christ and what is destined to happen to those, whoever they may be, who are in Christ.[73]

Justifiably Apostle Paul uses corporate language to describe the Christian's election. Therefore, the proposition is advanced that election is corporate and is applicable to the Church. Predestination is applicable to the privileges and purposes of God's creative design and Christological mandate for the Church. To suggest that the names of the elect were written in the Lamb's book of life before the foundation of the world (individualistic determinism) is fallacious. This interpretation would posit the argument that they were saved at that moment. The conclusion to be drawn from this teaching would present the contradiction of being saved and being under the condemnation of sin at the same time. Furthermore, the issue of the literal, figurative, or metaphysical pre-existence of the soul rears its ugly head. An excellent way to summarize effectively corporate election and eliminate unbiblical postulates of unconditional election would be to advocate, "The election of Christ, the pre-existent corporate head of the Church, before the foundation of the world entails the election of the Church because he is the corporate head and representative of the Church, and what is true of him as their representative is also true of them, his body."[74]

The Predestination of Spiritual Blessings

Ephesians 1:1-14 is a powerful text that declares the rich spiritual blessings that God predestinated for His church. Before addressing the enumeration of these blessings it should be noted that nothing in all these predestinated spiritual blessings for the church, according to theologian John Miley:

[73] Ben Witherington III, *The Problem with Evangelical Theology* (Waco: Baylor University Press, 2005), 84

[74] Abasciano, "Clearing up Misconceptions about Corporate Election," 70.

either expresses or implies an absolute personal election to salvation ... there is nothing in all this contrary to the truest conditionality of salvation; nothing in proof of an absolute predestination of a definite part of mankind to final blessedness, with the consequent reprobation of the rest to an inevitable penal doom.[75]

I. Howard Marshall, in accordance with Miley, finds that nothing in the text suggests unconditional election: "All that we are told is that God foreordains those who believe to become holy and to be His sons."[76] God, before the foundation of the world, predestinated that all who accept Jesus Christ as their personal Savior, by faith in His shed blood, would enjoy many spiritual blessings. First, in Ephesians 1:4, God predestinated a spotless, pure church that would be separated unto Him and through sanctification believers would be conformed to the image of Christ. The purpose was that the church must be morally, ethically, and spiritually free from condemnation to show forth the love of God. Paul reiterated this truth elsewhere: "That he might present it to himself a glorious church, not having spot, or wrinkle, or any such thing; but that it should be holy and without blemish" (Ephesians 5:27).

A second predestinated spiritual blessing is the adoption of sonship signifying the privileges and rights of family relationships. This blessing is possible through the redemptive work of Jesus Christ on the cross (Ephesians 1:7), where sins are forgiven of the repentant believer. Paul reinforced this theme later in the book of Ephesians: "Now therefore ye are no more strangers and foreigners, but fellow-citizens with the saints, and of the household of God" (Ephesians 2:19).

A third predestinated spiritual blessing is the acceptance in the beloved given to the believer "to the praise of the glory of his grace"

---

[75] John Miley, *Systematic Theology-Volume II* (Peabody, MA: Hendrickson Publisher, 1989), 262-263.
[76] Marshall, *Kept by the Power of God*, 104.

(Ephesians 1:6). The exaltation of the character of Christ and the compliment of His grace establish the foundational premise of true praise in the finished work of Jesus Christ through His crucifixion and resurrection. The privilege and joy to reveal His precepts, magnify His person, and manifest His power while in this present world will finally consummate in eschatological surety. Paul repeated this teaching in Ephesians 1:12 where he wrote, "That we should be to the praise of his glory, who first trusted in Christ."

A fourth predestinated spiritual blessing is the "mystery of his will" (Ephesians 1:9). First Corinthians 2:14 serves as a preface to understanding the spiritual blessing. "But the natural man receiveth not the things of the Spirit of God: for they are foolishness unto him: neither can he know them, because they are spiritually discerned." With the guidance of the Holy Spirit in interpreting the Scriptures, the unfolding of dispensational revelation with its typologies, prophecies, and divine interventions finds it purpose in the fulfillment of Jesus Christ. Paul revealed this theme in Ephesians 3:9, where he wrote, "And to make all men see what is the fellowship of the mystery, which from the beginning of the world hath been hid in God, who created all things by Jesus Christ."

A fifth predestinated spiritual blessing for the saints is an 'obtained inheritance" (Ephesians 1:11). The word inheritance conveys the meaning of portion or heritage. A proper understanding of this verse is connected to the eschatological ending of v.10. Although one enjoys the provisions of salvation in Christ daily, the focus is on the promise of the eternal destiny when this life has ended. Peter sheds light on this Scripture. While we are kept by the power of God, Peter noted that we have "an inheritance incorruptible, and undefiled, and that fadeth not away, reserved in heaven for you" (1 Peter 1:4). Paul continued his focus on the inheritance reserved for the saints by appealing to the Holy Spirit. He incorporated the present and the future by declaring that the Holy Spirit of promise is the evidence of regeneration and a declaration of ownership of the church. In addition, the promise of heaven is also guaranteed by the Holy Spirit of promise. Ephesians 1:14 confirms both of these statements:

"Which is the earnest of our inheritance until the redemption of the purchased possession, unto the praise of his glory." At this point one can readily answer the question as to what is predestinated in Ephesians 1:1-14. Clearly, the spiritual blessings of the Christian life and not the predestinated individualistic salvation of unconditional election is the focus of this passage. Free will is involved and is even discussed in this very same chapter: "In whom ye also trusted, after that ye heard the word of truth, the gospel of your salvation: in whom also after that ye believed, ye were sealed with the holy Spirit of promise" (Ephesians 1:13).

Concluding Comments on Unconditional Election

The purpose of this chapter has been to expose the fallacious and damnable teaching of unconditional election. To achieve this goal, Ephesians 1:1-14 has been examined. Several conclusions have been reached as a result of this careful investigation. The chief observation, however, is that Paul presents election and predestination as Christocentric and corporate. Thus, because Paul's primary focus is on the corporate body of Christ, and what God has determined for this corporate entity, unconditional election, as taught by Calvinists, is shown to be a fictitious biblical position. In this final section comments will be offered by different scholars and theologians to further refute the erroneous doctrine of unconditional election.

It requires biblical and exegetical gymnastics in order to reach the conclusion that God has predestined some people to be eternally saved and other people to be eternally damned. To achieve such an erroneous and preposterous position, one must divide the omnipotence, omniscience, omni-benevolence, and omni-sapience, as well as other attributes of God, into categories to justify the unbiblical teaching to prevent a sovereign God from violating and contradicting His own nature. Noted theologian Frank Stagg remarked, "God's favor does not imply favoritism. It knows no 'double predestination' (i.e., some predestinated to salvation and some to damnation), nor does it know an arbitrary salvation imposed without moral change or imposed without faith. The New Testament knows no 'irresistible grace.'"[77] In Psalms 98:9 the Bible says the Lord "cometh to judge the earth: *with righteousness shall he judge the world, and the people with equity*." The saintly John Wesley, when commenting on the righteous justice of God, noted:

> He will punish no man for doing anything which he could not possibly avoid; neither for omitting anything which he could not possibly do. Every punishment supposes the offender might have avoided the offense for which he is punished: otherwise, to punish him would be palpably unjust, and inconsistent with the character of God our Governor.[78]

In addition, as Austin Fischer observed, "If one believes that God unconditionally ordained 'the elect' to eternal salvation and the 'non-elect' to eternal damnation then a paradoxical dilemma is created as to the understanding of God's love, justice, and goodness."[79] Influential Anglican theologian Charles Gore stated that "the idea of a predestination for good, taking effect necessarily and irrespective of men's co-operation, is an idea which has been intruded unjustifiably into St. Paul's thought."[80] He also insisted, "That God should create any single individual with the intention of eternally destroying or punishing him is a horrible idea, and, without prying into mysteries, we may say boldly that there is no warrant for it in the Old or New Testaments."[81] Finally, God has sovereignly

---

[77] Stagg, *New Testament Theology*, 84.

[78] John Wesley, *The Works of John Wesley- Vol. X* (Grand Rapids, MI: Baker Book House, 1978), 363.

[79] Austin Fischer, *Young Restless, No Longer Reformed* (Eugene, OR: Cascade Books, 2014), 35.

[80] Charles Gore, *The Epistle to the Ephesians* (London, England: John Murray, Albemarble St., 1898), 66.

[81] Ibid., 64.

willed that salvation comes through faith. Norman Geisler explains how this relates to God's essence: "Faith is a free act on the part of the recipient, for an omnibenevolent God must not only love all, but He must respect the freedom He freely gave to His creatures. It is necessary for God to act in accordance with His own perfect nature, and love is of this very essence."[82]

---

[82] Geisler, *Systematic Theology in One Volume*, 827.

CHAPTER 3

Reprobation and Romans 9

A key distinguishing feature of Calvinism is its doctrine of reprobation. Reformed theologian Wayne Grudem defines reprobation as "the sovereign decision of God before creation to pass over some persons, in sorrow deciding not to save them, and to punish them for their sins, and thereby to manifest his justice."[83] This belief that God has chosen certain individuals for eternal damnation is "the necessary corollary to the doctrine of unconditional election,"[84] as Grudem himself admits: "When we understand election as God's sovereign choice of some persons to be saved, then *there is necessarily another aspect of that choice*, namely, God's sovereign decision to pass over others and not to save them."[85] Thus, because Calvinists define election as "an act of God in which he chooses some people to be saved, not on account of any foreseen

---

[83] Wayne Grudem, *Systematic Theology* (Grand Rapids, MI: Zondervan, 1994), 684.

[84] Eric Hankins, "Romans 9 and the Calvinist Doctrine of Reprobation," *JBTM* 15 (2018): 62.

[85] Grudem, *Systematic Theology*, 684. Italics mine.

merit in them, but only because of his sovereign good pleasure,"[86] the necessary inference from this position is that there is a group of people not chosen for salvation because God decided, before creation, "not to save them."

Most Calvinists recognize the awfulness of reprobation. Grudem, for instance, acknowledged:

> The doctrine of reprobation is the most difficult of all the teachings of Scripture for us to think about and to accept, because it deals with such horrible and eternal consequences for human beings made in the image of God. The love that God gives us for our fellow human beings and the love that he commands us to have toward our neighbor cause us to recoil against this doctrine, and it is right that we feel such dread in contemplating it.[87]

However, even though this conviction that God has unconditionally chosen to damn certain persons to hell causes even those who believe in it to tremble in fear, *Calvinists believe in reprobation because they think that the Scriptures teach it.* Grudem, again, writes, "It is something that we would not want to believe, and would not believe, unless Scripture clearly taught it ... If we are convinced that these verses teach reprobation, then we are obligated both to believe it and accept it as fair and just of God, even though it still cause us to tremble in horror as we think of it."[88] Fortunately, Christians do not have to be "convinced that these verses teach reprobation."

Where does Grudem, along with other Calvinists, think that the Bible teaches unconditional reprobation of certain individuals to eternal damnation? Romans 9 is the main source of support used

---

[86] Ibid., 670.

[87] Ibid., 684-685.

[88] Ibid., 685.

to construct the erroneous doctrine of reprobation.[89] A brief look at this passage explains how Calvinists see reprobation taught:

> And not only this; but when Rebecca also had conceived by one, even by our father Isaac; (for the children being not yet born, neither having done any good or evil, that the purpose of God according to election might stand, not of works, but of him that calleth;) it was said unto her, The elder shall serve the younger. As it is written, Jacob have I loved, but Esau have I hated … For he saith to Moses, I will have mercy on whom I will have mercy, and I will have compassion on whom I will have compassion. So then it is not of him that willeth, nor of him that runneth, but of God that sheweth mercy. For the scripture saith unto Pharaoh, Even for this same purpose have I raised thee up, that I might shew my power in thee, and that my name might be declared throughout all the earth. Therefore hath he mercy on whom he will have mercy, and whom he will he hardeneth (Romans 9:10-13;15-18).

In examining these verses, Robert Shank's admission is understandable: "There is full warrant for Calvin's doctrine of unconditional particular election and reprobation in Romans 9:6-29 *if it is considered 'alone' and is accepted as essentially all that the Bible has to say on the subject of election.*"[90] However, as Shank continued, "No passage of Scripture stands in isolation from its context, and the context of Romans 9:6-29 forbids the conclusions that Calvin

---

[89] Also frequently employed by Calvinists are 1 Peter 2:8 and Jude 4. Hankins is correct in his analysis of these verses: "There is every reason to understand that these verses as simply pointing out the fact that God has always planned to condemn those who oppose the gospel" ("Romans 9 and the Calvinist Doctrine of Reprobation," 65).

[90] Shank, *Elect in the Son*, 115. Italics mine.

drew from the passage."[91] In a little bit, we will conduct an analysis of this passage and demonstrate that "the problematic doctrine of reprobation is not a necessary theological implication of Romans 9."[92] First, however, it is essential to point out an initial error of the Calvinistic understanding of Romans 9.

In studying the Scriptures, you can be confident in the fact that one portion of the Bible will *never* contradict another portion of the Bible. Our interpretations of certain passages might be flawed and in need of improvement, but the Bible is perfect, the inspired word of God that does not error. Therefore, it is utterly impossible for the Scriptures to teach two contradictory principles. If the Bible clearly teaches a certain truth repeatedly throughout, yet a few passages seem to contradict this truth, we must evaluate those apparently contradictory passages in light of God's clear revelation.

One of the clearest truths in the Scriptures is that God desires the salvation of everyone. Paul wrote that God "will have all men to be saved, and to come unto the knowledge of the truth" (1 Timothy 2:4). He announced elsewhere that "the grace of God that bringeth salvation hath appeared to all men" (Titus 2:11). His comments concerning God's universal saving will are confirmed by the Apostle Peter, who informed his readers that God "is longsuffering to us-ward, not willing that any should perish, but that all should come to repentance" (2 Peter 3:9). The prophet Ezekiel described the Lord's anguish over the death of the wicked: "Have I any pleasure at all that the wicked should die? saith the Lord God: and not that he should return from his ways, and live?" (Ezekiel 18:23). These sentiments are perhaps best expressed in the familiar words of Jesus: "For God so loved the world, that he gave his only begotten Son, that whosoever believeth in him should not perish, but have everlasting life" (John 3:16). So, according to the Scriptures, God loves the world; is not pleased with the death of the wicked; wants all men to be saved; and is not willing that any should perish, but that all should come to repentance. These are clear, unequivocal statements that affirm

---

[91] Ibid.

[92] Hankins, "Romans 9 and the Calvinist Doctrine of Reprobation," 65.

God's unquestionable desire for the salvation of all people. And, as Shank observed, "Recognition of the will of God for the salvation of all men completely negates Calvin's system of theology."[93]

How, then, does this relate to Romans 9 and the Calvinistic doctrine of reprobation? If God genuinely desires the salvation of all men, then reprobation is necessarily false, because reprobation implies that God does not desire the salvation of all men and decided, before creation, not to save all men.[94] Therefore, Romans 9, whatever it teaches, does not teach reprobation, since, as recognized above, Scripture cannot contradict Scripture. God desires the salvation of all men, while the Calvinist doctrine of reprobation, founded primarily upon a mistaken interpretation of Romans 9, insinuates that God does *not* desire the salvation of all men. These two positions are mutually exclusive, and the latter one ought to be rejected since the former one is confirmed throughout the infallible word of God. Roger Olson's advice is correct: "Scripture as a whole, and Jesus Christ in particular, identifies God as loving and just; if an individual passage (even a whole chapter) appears to contradict this, it must be interpreted in the light of the whole of revelation and not be allowed to dominate, control and ultimately overturn the true meaning of God's self disclosure as good."[95]

A basic syllogism can be formed to summarize the argument in the preceding paragraphs:

1. If God desires the salvation of all men, then reprobation is false.
2. God desires the salvation of all men.
3. Therefore, reprobation is false.

---

[93] Shank, *Elect in the Son*, 92.

[94] I write this fully aware of the Calvinistic distinction between God's secret will and God's revealed will. God's secret will is what he has determined to come to pass, while his revealed will is his moral law unveiled in the Scriptures. For example, his revealed will is that Christians should not commit sexual immorality (1 Thessalonians 4:3), although his secret will could be that certain Christians will necessarily commit sexual immorality.

[95] Olson, *Arminian Theology*, 110.

Let's now begin our study of Romans 9. We will look at some background information to the passage and then analyze Romans 9, highlighting further problems with the Calvinistic interpretation of this passage as we work our way through the text.

The Background of Romans 9

To the credit of Calvinists who have saturated the bookstores with their literature and the radio with their sermons, many Christians are intimidated by the word "election," thinking that only Calvinists believe in election. This, of course, is false, since the Bible teaches the concept of election. Every Christian ought to sincerely desire to understand just what the Bible means when it discusses this highly controversial topic.

In his book *The Love of God*, John Peckham explains that there are two kinds of election in the Bible: vocational election and salvific election.[96] He defines vocational election as "God's choice of individuals and/or groups for a specific role in the plan of salvation, often with the purpose of revealing God's character."[97] An example of this is Jesus's choice of twelve men from his disciples to be apostles: "And when it was day, [Jesus] called unto him his disciples: and of them he chose twelve, whom also he named apostles" (Luke 6:13).[98] Vocational election is not God's choice of people to be saved but his choice of people for service in his gracious plan of salvation. Interestingly, even unsaved people can be vocationally elected for a

---

[96] John C. Peckham, *The Love of God* (Downers Grove: IVP Academic, 2015), 101.

[97] Ibid.

[98] Similar to Luke 6:13 is John 15:16: "Ye have not chosen me, but I have chosen you..." The choice in view is Jesus' choice of certain of his disciples to be his apostles, not unsaved people to salvation. Robert Shank concurred: "The choice of which Christ speaks is to the Apostolate rather than to salvation (cf. Mk. 3:13ff., Lk. 6:13ff., Acts 1:2, etc.), a choice which Christ made among His larger body of disciples (Lk. 6:13)" (*Elect in the Son*, 180).

specific task. According to Ben Witherington III, "One can be chosen for God's purposes, like Cyrus or Pharaoh, and not be saved."[99]

Salvific election, on the other hand, "describes those instances in Scripture where those who will ultimately receive salvation are referred to as the 'elect.'"[100] According to the Bible, God chooses those in Christ (Ephesians 1:4) for salvation. In other words, God chooses believers, but he does not choose who will believe.[101] At any rate, salvific and vocational election are not synonymous. Theological problems arise when these two different types of election are conflated. Again, those vocationally elected are not necessarily salvifically elected.

Another example of vocational election is the election of Israel. Out of all the nations of the world, God chose Israel. Why did he choose Israel? Marston and Forster explain, "The whole election of the nation, as announced to Abraham, was with the object of preparing for a seed (Christ) through whom all nations would be blessed."[102] God did not choose the nation of Israel for salvation; instead, he chose them to be the vehicle through which all people would be blessed. Consider the words of the Lord to Abraham: "And I will make of thee a great nation, and I will bless thee, and make they name great; and *thou shalt be a blessing*: and I will bless them that bless thee, and curse him that curseth thee: and *in thee shall all families of the earth be blessed*" (Genesis 12:2,3). Marston and Forster, again, provide insight into what God's choice of Israel entailed: "The choice of Abraham and Israel was not merely for their own benefit; it was not a guarantee that all Jews would be saved; it was so that God could *through them* do something for the world."[103]

Therefore, when God elected Abraham and his descendants to be his people through which the promised seed would come

---

[99] Ben Witherington III, *Paul's Letter to the Romans* (Grand Rapids: Wm. B. Eerdmans, 2004), 255.

[100] Peckham, *The Love of God*, 102.

[101] See the chapter on Ephesians 1 for more information about salvific election.

[102] Marston and Forster, *God's Strategy in Human History*, 141.

[103] Ibid., 45. Italics mine.

(Genesis 3:15), he did not consequently choose to condemn the rest of the nations of the world. Charlie Trimm observes, "Israel's election did not automatically entail the condemnation of the other nations."[104] Lennox agrees, "God's choice of Israel as his people does not mean that everyone else was written off for condemnation."[105] Peckham's suggestion is terrific: "God's choice of a special people was not to the exclusion of others but toward blessing all nations (Genesis 12:2-3) … God's election of the few ultimately benefits all, since God intends, through Israel, to eventually enter into love relationship with people of all nations."[106] Simply put, God blessed Abraham so that he could be a blessing to "all families of the earth" (Genesis 12:2).

This brings us to Romans 9 and the problem that Paul is seeking to address in this portion of Scripture. The nation of Israel possesses (not possessed) the adoption, the law, the covenants, the service in the temple, and, above all, Christ (Romans 9:1-5). Nevertheless, in spite of this privileged position, a majority of the Israelites are not coming to faith in Jesus. They are rejecting him as their Messiah. For Paul, this Jewish unbelief is undermining "the credibility of the gospel he is preaching."[107] As John Taylor noted, "If the gospel of Israel's Messiah has not saved Israel, how can it be considered good news at all? If the Gentiles are joining in large numbers, but Jews are not, perhaps there is something fundamentally wrong with the message, and with the Gentile mission."[108] Austin Fischer's observation is helpful:

---

[104] Charlie Trimm, "Did YHWH Condemn the Nations When He Elected Israel? YHWH's Disposition toward Non-Israelites in the Torah," *JETS* 55 (2012): 536.

[105] Lennox, *Determined to Believe?*, 242.

[106] Peckham, *The Love of God*, 106.

[107] Hankins, "Romans 9 and the Calvinist Doctrine of Reprobation," 65.

[108] John W. Taylor, "The Freedom of God and the Hope of Israel: Theological Interpretation of Romans," *Southwestern Journal of Theology* 56 (2013): 36.

All that Paul has said up until this point [in Romans]-about the impartiality of God, about the people of God being Jew and Gentile united in Christ, about the inadequacy and obsoleteness of the Law, about all coming to God on the basis of grace and faith in Jesus the Messiah- has *begged the question of Israel*. Why has Israel, by and large, rejected its Messiah? What is God doing with Israel? Has he forsaken his first chosen people (Israel) for a new chosen people (Gentiles)? If so, hasn't God been unfaithful to his promises to Israel?[109]

In Romans 9-11, Paul is attempting to address the reason why the vast majority of the nation of Israel is rejecting the gospel of Jesus Christ. Thus, as Lennox comments, "Paul's concern in Romans 9-11 is not the basis of the gospel but why it is that the very nation that was privileged by God to be the vehicle of his revelation to the world now mainly rejects the gospel of the Messiah."[110] Walls and Dongell are of the same opinion as Lennox: "These three chapters, properly read together, address not so much the question of how *individuals* are saved …, but rather what Christians should say about Israel in light of its current rejection of the gospel."[111] When the centrality of Jewish unbelief in the gospel is seen as the central concern for Paul in these chapters, it becomes apparent that "Romans 9-11 is focused on *the salvation-historical role of unbelieving Jews in the present*, not *the ontological status of all unbelieving people for all time*."[112]

An Analysis of Romans 9:6-23

Paul begins with his own conclusion: the word of God has not failed (v. 6)! To support his conclusion, he retells "Israel's history,

---

[109] Fischer, *Young, Restless, No Longer Reformed*, 100. Italics his.

[110] Lennox, *Determined to Believe?*, 240.

[111] Walls and Dongell, *Why I Am Not a Calvinist*, 85.

[112] Hankins, "Romans 9 and the Calvinist Doctrine of Reprobation," 65.

illustrating that from start to finish the faithfulness and mercy of God have been stronger than the faithlessness of Israel."[113] The first part of this history lesson involves Abraham and Isaac. Paul writes:

> For they are not all Israel, which are of Israel: Neither, because they are the seed of Abraham, are they all children: but, In Isaac shall thy seed be called. That is, They which are the children of the flesh, these are not the children of God: but the children of the promise are counted for the seed. For this is the word of promise, At this time will I come, and Sarah shall have a son (Romans 9:6-9).

What, then, is Paul's primary point in this portion of Scripture? Not all the descendants of Abraham were chosen to carry the seed of the Messiah. Abraham had two sons: Isaac and Ishmael. In a very real way, Ishmael, just like Isaac, was the seed of Abraham. However, it was "in Isaac" that Abraham's seed would be named (9:8). Marston and Forster explain well the difference between Isaac and Ishmael: "The great and only distinction is that *from Isaac* would spring the nation whose Messiah would bring world-wide blessing."[114] Importantly, God's choice of Isaac, instead of Ishmael, did not involve his eternal destiny; it was about his special role to play in Israel's history. John Lennox again provides powerful insight:

> We should notice that this text has nothing to do with the personal salvation of Isaac ... The statement that Isaac was a child of promise is not made in connection with his personal, spiritual birth through faith in God, but his physical birth through the faith of Abraham and Sarah. God's selection of

---

[113] Fischer, *Young, Restless, No Longer Reformed*, 101.

[114] Marston and Forster, *God's Strategy in Human History*, 46. Italics mine.

Isaac as the seed through whom he would fulfill his promise to bless the world was a sovereign choice.[115]

Lennox's observation that this passage does not address the personal salvation of Isaac can be strengthened by considering two factors. First, Paul's quotation in v. 9 of Genesis 18:10 demonstrates what the children of promise is about: "Sarah shall have a son." According to Scripture, Sarah could not have children, so she devised a scheme for fulfilling God's promise to Abraham. She prompted Abraham to have a child through her servant Hagar. Abraham complied with his wife's wishes, and Ishmael was conceived as a result of Abraham and Hagar's union. This, of course, was in violation of God's will. God desired for Abraham and Sarah to trust him to fulfill his promises, not to try to fulfill them through their own efforts. Thus, Isaac was a child of promise, not a child of the flesh, in the sense of being the "promised" child of a barren mother, through whom Christ would come, not in the sense of salvation.

Second, the Bible does *not* indicate that Ishmael was viewed as unacceptable in God's sight. Consider a conversation between Abraham and God in which Abraham intercedes on behalf of Ishmael:

> Abraham said unto God, O that Ishmael might live before thee! And God said, Sarah they wife shall bear thee a son indeed; and thou shalt call his name Isaac: and I will establish my covenant with him for an everlasting covenant, and with his seed after him. And *as for Ishmael, I have heard thee: Behold, I have blessed him*, and will make him fruitful, and will multiply him exceedingly; twelve princes shall he beget, and I will make him a great nation (Genesis 17:18-20).

Notice that the text explicitly states that God has blessed Ishmael. Obviously, God had a special plan for Isaac and his seed. However,

---

[115] Lennox, Determined to Believe?, 245.

God did not curse Ishmael just because he chose to bless Isaac with the privilege of carrying the seed for the Messiah. Romans 9 is discussing God's sovereign choice of Isaac, instead of Ishmael, to "carry the seed-line of the Messiah in the physical sense."[116] This passage is not about the unconditional election of Isaac to salvation and the unconditional reprobation of Ishmael. The use of this Romans 9:6-9 to teach the erroneous doctrine of unconditional election is an egregious example of taking the Bible out of context.

Paul considers the next generation:

> And not only this; but when Rebecca also had conceived by one, even by our father Isaac; (For the children being not yet born, neither having done any good or evil, that the purpose of God according to election might stand, not of works, but of him that calleth;) it was said unto her, The elder shall serve the younger. As it is written, Jacob have I loved, but Esau have I hated (Romans 9:10-13).

He writes that before either had been born or had done good or evil, God said unto Rebecca, "The elder shall serve the younger." Some comments need to be made in order to demonstrate that Paul's "concern is with roles they are to play in history, not their personal eternal destiny."[117] For starters, the purpose of the election of Jacob, not Esau, is so that the older son (Esau) would serve the younger son (Jacob). Nothing here suggests that the salvation of Jacob is the object of God's choice. Klein's explanation is worth observing: "God did not base his choice of Jacob over Esau on any works either of them had done or left undone. God simply made a sovereign decision to appoint Jacob for his role in the line of the patriarchs ... Therefore I doubt that this appointment concerns Jacob's personal salvation."[118]

---

[116] Ibid., 244.

[117] Witherington III, *Paul's Letter to the Romans*, 254.

[118] Klein, *The New Chosen People*, 175-176.

What is sometimes overlooked in various interpretations of this passage is that Paul is primarily talking about nations, not just individuals. Considering the Old Testament context from which Paul quotes proves this contention:

> And the Lord said unto her, *Two nations* are in thy womb, and two manner of people shall be separated from thy bowels; and the one people shall be stronger than the other people; and the elder shall serve younger (Genesis 25:23).

Quite obviously, Jacob and Esau represent two different nations. Importantly, Esau himself never did serve Jacob. Marston and Forster comment, "Esau the individual certainly did not serve Jacob, it was the nation Esau (or Edom) which served the nation Jacob (or Israel)."[119] Thus, if Romans 9:12 is taken to refer *only* to individuals, then the Bible contains contradictory information, since Esau never did serve Jacob. The resolution to this quandary, of course, is that the Lord's words to Sarah, from which Paul quotes, refer *primarily* to nations, not to individuals. God chose Jacob and his descendants, instead of Esau and his, to play an important part in God's strategy to bring redemption to the world.

Paul's final remark about Jacob and Esau in Romans 9 is a reference to Malachi 1:2,3. Again, context demonstrates that Malachi is concerned more with the nation of Jacob than the nation of Esau. So, the Lord loved the nation of Israel but hated the nation of Esau. What does this mean? Did God literally hate the descendants of Esau? Marston and Forster are correct:

> When the Bible uses the word hate as a contrast to love, it intends us to understand it to mean 'love less than' ... The verse does not mean that in a literal hatred of Esau and his descendants God has condemned every one of them to hell. It has reference

---

[119] Marston and Forster, *God's Strategy in Human History*, 51.

simply to the higher position of the Hebrew race in the strategy of God.[120]

The words of Christ give a good illustration of what "hate" means in Malachi 1:3. Jesus declared, "If any man come to me, and hate not his father, and mother, and wife, and children, and brethren, and sisters, yea, and his own life also, he cannot be my disciple" (Luke 14:26). Did Jesus literally command those who desired to be his disciples to hate their family members? Of course not. Every serious student of the Bible knows that a wooden interpretation of Jesus's command would result in biblical contradictions. For instance, Paul commanded husbands to "love your wives" (Ephesians 5:25). Jesus said to hate our wives, and Paul demanded that we love our wives. Who is right? Both Jesus and Paul are right. The solution to this dilemma is to observe that Jesus commands his disciples to love everyone else, including those who are closest, less than they love him.

The same principle applies to Romans 9:13. Joseph Thayer acknowledged, "Ro. ix. 13, the signification *to love less, to postpone in love* or *esteem, to slight.*"[121] The conclusion of Marston and Forster is spot on: "God's 'love of Jacob but hatred of Esau' means this: God has chosen to give to the nation of Israel a special place and privileged position. This is not because of their 'works' for the passage that affirms his choice also proclaims their sinfulness. Rather, his choice is a result purely of his own strategy."[122]

Expecting opposition to what he has just said, Paul responds to a rhetorical question: "What shall we say then? Is there unrighteousness with God? God forbid" (Romans 9:14). The hypothetical objection challenged the justice and integrity of God. Was God's reputation tarnished because he chose Isaac and Jacob, not Ishmael and Esau? Was his righteousness impaired by his decision to bestow privileges

---

[120] Ibid., 53.

[121] Joseph H. Thayer, *Thayer's Greek-English Lexicon of the New Testament* (Peabody: Hendrickson Publishers, 2000), 415

[122] Marston and Forster, *God's Strategy in Human History*, 53.

on the nation of Israel regardless of their good works? Surely, these complaints had to be considered in light of Abraham's confident inquiry: "Shall not the Judge of all the earth do right?" (Genesis 18:25). Paul's initial reply to these rhetorical questions is to "roundly repudiate[] the suggestion"[123] that there is injustice with God. He then proceeds to further answer these questions by giving two historical examples from Israel's history that preserves God's impeccable righteousness and demonstrates that "He is free to bestow favors on some, and to deny them to others, without becoming answerable to any creature."[124] He continues:

> For he saith to Moses, I will have mercy on whom I will have mercy, and I will have compassion on whom I will have compassion. So then it is not of him that willeth, nor of him that runneth, but of God that sheweth mercy. For the scripture saith unto Pharaoh, Even for this same purpose have I raised thee up, that I might shew my power in thee, and that my name might be declared throughout all the earth. Therefore hath he mercy on whom he will have mercy, and whom he will he hardeneth (Romans 9:15-18).

Paul's first illustration of God's sovereign prerogative in human history involves Moses, the golden calf, and the nation of Israel. Many Christians are familiar with this despicable incident in the history of Israel. While their leader Moses is on top of Mount Sinai, receiving revelation from God, the nation is rebelling against God: "When the people saw that Moses delayed to come down out of the mount, the people gathered themselves together unto Aaron, and said unto him, Up, *make us gods*" (Exodus 32:1). The Lord's initial reaction to this blatant idolatry was to destroy the entire nation of Israel and create a new nation from Moses: "I have seen this people,

---

[123] Witherington III, *Paul's Letter to the Romans*, 256.

[124] Shank, *Elect in the Son*, 117.

and, behold, it is a stiffnecked people: now therefore let me alone, that my wrath may wax hot against them, and that I may consume them: and I will make of thee a great nation" (Exodus 32:9,10). Moses responds to God's harsh reaction to Israel's idolatry by interceding on their behalf. He prayed:

> Lord, why doth thy wrath wax hot against thy people, which thou hast brought forth out of the land of Egypt with great power, and with a mighty hand? Wherefore should the Egyptians speak, and say, For mischief did he bring them out, to slay them in the mountains, and to consume them from the face of the earth? Turn from thy fierce wrath, and repent of this evil against thy people. Remember Abraham, Isaac, and Israel, thy servants, to whom thou swarest by thine own self, and said unto them, I will multiply your seed as the stars of heaven, and all this land that I have spoken of will I give unto your seed, and they shall inherit it for ever. And *the Lord repented of the evil which he thought to do unto his people* (Exodus 32:11-14).

God intended to destroy Israel because of her stiffneckedness, yet he changed his mind in response to Moses' intercession. Instead of judgment, God had mercy on Israel. Before continuing our discussion of God's sovereign right to show mercy to whomever he desires, it might be helpful to consider how the previous biblical story portrays the type of God represented in the Bible. The words of Marston and Forster are powerful:

> This whole passage is certainly not about some implacable, unchanging, emotionless, timeless God who determines everything that happens. It is about a *personal* God who talks things over with his friend Moses, and *reacts* to both sin and intercession ... Our

> God is a powerful God, who upholds the universe
> by his word of power moment by moment, but who
> also *acts* as a participant within its history. Our
> God is a personal God, who feels emotion, volition,
> disappointment, and *reacts* in turn to human actions
> and reactions- sometimes changing his mind.[125]

Moses interceded on behalf of Israel, and God responded to his request by delaying judgment. In the next chapter, Moses continued to plead with the Lord, asking for God to "shew me thy glory" (Exodus 33:18). The Lord replied: "I will make all my goodness pass before thee, and I will proclaim the name of the Lord before thee; and will be gracious to whom I will be gracious, and will shew mercy on whom I will shew mercy" (Exodus 33:19). This last past is what Paul quotes in Romans 9:15.

So, what is Paul's emphasis at this point in his argument that God's word has not failed? It is God's right to grant mercy to a sinful nation instead of rightfully destroying them for their gross idolatry. Lennox's keen observation is precise: "Because of Israel's sin at this juncture of history, God would have been justified in destroying them. They did not deserve pardon, but in his mercy and compassion God gave it to them."[126] God knows best how and when to bestow mercy, just as he showed mercy, historically, in the election of the nation of Jacob. Ultimately, his demonstration of mercy is not dependent on "him that willeth, nor of him that runneth, but of God that sheweth mercy" (Romans 9:16). His choice of Jacob, not Esau, did not depend on anything in the particular individual. His decision to spare the nation of Israel because of Moses' intercession is his prerogative. As Marston and Forster conclude, "God's strategy is not determined by human volition or effort. He reacts to human choice, but cannot be dictated to."[127]

Paul resumes his defense of God's justice by introducing Pharaoh

[125] Marston and Forster, *God's Strategy in Human History*, 59, 342

[126] Lennox, *Determined to Believe?*, 255.

[127] Marston and Forster, *God's Strategy in Human History*, 61.

into the discussion. He has just demonstrated God's right to show mercy to a people undeserving of it. Now, he will argue that it is also within God's authority to harden someone who rebels against his will: "For the scripture saith unto Pharaoh, Even for this same purpose have I raised thee up, that I might shew my power in thee, and that my name might be declared throughout all the earth" (Romans 9:17). Examining the context of Paul's quotation about Pharaoh will prove to be useful in understanding what Paul is intending to communicate to his readers. He quotes from Exodus 9:

> The Lord said unto Moses, Rise up early in the morning, and stand before Pharaoh, and say unto him, Thus saith the Lord God of the Hebrews, Let my people go, that they may serve me. For I will at this time send all my plagues upon thine heart, and upon thy servants, and upon thy people; that thou mayest know that there is none like me in all the earth. For now I will stretch out my hand, that I may smite thee and thy people with pestilence; and thou shalt be cut off from the earth. And in very deed *for this cause have I raised thee up, for to shew in thee my power; and that my name may be declared throughout all the earth* (Exodus 9:13-16).

A few comments must be made about God's hardening of Pharaoh and Paul's quotation. First, the "raising up" of Pharaoh does not refer to his birth; it refers to God's preserving him from death in order to display his power through Pharaoh's stubbornness. Consider the explanation of Everett Harrison:

> "I raised you up" is not strictly a reference to Pharaoh's emergence in history but to God's providence in sparing him up to that time. Pharaoh deserved death for his oppression and insolence, but his life would not be taken during the series

of plagues, so that the full extent of his hardness of heart might be evident and the glory of God in the deliverance of his people enhanced in all the earth.[128]

Ben Witherington III concurs:

Pharaoh was raised up to demonstrate God's saving power on behalf of Israel and thus to show the glory of God throughout the earth. That he was judged or hardened is a byproduct, but God acted to redeem his people. It is a regular feature of God's work that redemption for one person may require or involve judgment on another person. Liberation of the oppressed requires judgment of the oppressor. Nothing is said about Pharaoh's eternal state, but rather only how he was used by God during the exodus. "Raise up" does not refer to resurrection here, but rather to God bringing Pharaoh onto the stage of history and hardening him to reveal his mercy and power to save Israel.[129]

Pharaoh was not an innocent bystander, peaceably coexisting alongside the Israelites without causing them any trouble. As Walls and Dongell note, "It is apparent that God did not transform Pharaoh from a meek and mild gentleman to the fire-breathing dragon Moses met; rather God strengthened Pharaoh's heart in the perverse direction Pharaoh himself had already resolutely chosen."[130] There is an observable progression in the narrative of Pharaoh's life. He was opposed to the things of God. Then, God encouraged that

---

[128] Tremper Longman III and David E. Garland, *The Expositor's Bible Commentary-Volume 11* (Grand Rapids: Zondervan, 2006), 153.

[129] Witherington III, *Paul's Letter to the Romans*, 257.

[130] Walls and Dongell, *Why I Am Not a Calvinist*, 89.

stiffneckedness so that his power would be shown and his name would be declared throughout all the earth (Exodus 9:16). This hardening of Pharaoh's heart, however, did not make it impossible for him to repent and believe God; rather, the hardening confirmed Pharaoh's stubbornness so that Pharaoh would behave in a manner that was contrary to sound reason. Marston and Forster contend, "What God did was to confirm Pharaoh in the path he had chosen and strengthen his resolve to act on his evil inclinations even when sheer prudent self-interest would have militated against it."[131]

What is Paul's point, then, in talking about God's mercy to Moses and his hardening of Pharaoh's heart? He is arguing that it is God's right to have mercy on whom he wants to have mercy and to harden whom he wants to harden (Romans 9:18). Clearly, however, he is not talking about the eternal destiny of individuals that God decided before the world began. In context, Paul maintains that God knows best how to distribute mercy and judgment in order to accomplish his overarching purposes. Just like with the nation of Israel, he can show mercy to them despite their rampant idolatry, or he can show judgment, as he did when he hardened Pharaoh's heart. In both instances, God's actions served to further his grand, glorious purpose of blessing all the nations of the world through Israel. The wisdom and warning of Paul Achtemeier is worthy of close inspection:

> Considered in isolation, or against the background of the fate of individuals, these verses will almost inevitably be misunderstood. The difficulty lies in the fact that those who have understood these verses to be statements of eternal truth about how God deals with each individual, rather than a statement of how God has dealt with Israel in pursuing his plan for the redemption of his rebellious creation, have also tended to understand these verses in terms of a rigid and symmetrical predeterminism.

---

[131] Marston and Forster, *God's Strategy in Human History*, 261.

In such a predeterminism, God had determined before each individual was born whether or not that person would be saved or damned. Nothing that individual could do would alter that fact. Those who were damned got what they deserved as rebellious creatures. Those who were saved were saved only by grace. But the symmetry of grace and wrath was unbroken: As God acted in grace toward some persons, he acted in wrath toward others. That is simply not what Paul is saying in this passage. He is not writing about the fate of each individual. He is making a statement about how God dealt with Israel, and continues to deal with it, even when it rejects his Son; namely, he deals with it in mercy, even when it deserves wrath. That is why one so badly distorts Paul's point if one assumes these verses tell me about my fate, or anyone else's, before God: damned or saved. Rather, what these verses tell me is that the same gracious purpose at work in the election of Israel is now at work in a new chosen people to whom I can now also belong, by that same gracious purpose of God. The passage is therefore about the enlargement of God's mercy to include gentiles, not about the narrow and predetermined fate of each individual. We gentiles can now be part of his gracious purpose, we can be part of his people, chosen by grace through Christ Jesus. *That* is the point of this passage.[132]

Interestingly, then, Paul holds up the illustration of Pharaoh as analogous to what he is doing, in a sense, to the rebellious nation of Israel. In our chapter about John 6, we discussed the reality that the nation of Israel, because of their stubborn rebellion, was being

---

[132] Paul J. Achtemeier, *Romans: Interpretation: A Bible Commentary for Teaching and Preaching* (Louisville: Westminster John Knox Press, 2010), 165

hardened by God for the particular purpose of bringing redemption to both Jews and Gentiles. Thus, in reminding his readers about what God did to Pharaoh in order for his name to be "declared throughout all the earth" (Romans 9:17), he is also bringing attention to God's temporary hardening of Israel (Romans 11:25). Glen Shellrude makes this connection: "In the past God was able to use a 'hardened Pharaoh' to manifest his power and ensure a broad proclamation of his name. In the present God uses the occasion of a hardened Israel to accomplish another good, i.e. the proclamation of the Gospel to the Gentiles."[133]

This proclamation of the gospel amongst the Gentiles is not described in detail here by Paul. However, the story of the good news of Jesus Christ changing the lives of the heathens throughout the world is presented in the book of Acts. The apostles and evangelists often tried to convert Jews to Christ. Unfortunately, these attempts resulted in hostile reactions from the Jewish people, who attempted to murder many of these valiant disciples of the Messiah. This aggressive rejection of the gospel led the early Christians to begin to evangelize the Gentiles. Walls and Dongell describe this beautifully: "Jewish resistance to the gospel formed, in effect, a bridge the apostles and evangelists crossed to evangelize the nations of the world. God transformed their resistance into opportunity."[134] In essence, God used the rejection of the Jewish people as a means of bestowing "mercy upon all" (Romans 11:32). He responded to the Jewish people's unwillingness to submit themselves to the righteousness of God (Romans 10:3) by giving "them the spirit of slumber, eyes that they should not see, and ears that they should not hear" (Romans 11:8), so that the gospel would also be preached to the Gentiles.

Was it impossible for the Jewish people to be saved? Of course not. The hardness that had come upon the Israelites was temporary. As Eric Hankins writes, "Paul will make the point in Rom 11:25 that this hardening of unbelieving Jews will last only until all the

---

[133] Glen Shellrude, "The freedom of God in mercy and judgment: a libertarian reading of Romans 9:6-29," *EQ* 81 (2009): 313.
[134] Walls and Dongell, *Why I Am Not a Calvinist*, 90.

'fullness' of the Gentiles is achieved, then these unbelieving Jews will be saved, if they believe."[135] Further, the present hardening refers to Israel, nationally, not to individual Israelites. Shank agrees, "During the present lapse of Israel, nationally, the salvation of individuals, both Jews and Gentiles ([Romans] 10:12,13), remains a separate and distinct consideration, entirely independent of the question of the circumstance of Israel, nationally."[136] Paul himself is an example that God has not "cast away his people" (Romans 11:2). Even though Paul knows that through Israel's stumbling salvation has come to the Gentiles, Israel's fall is not irrevocable (Romans 11:11). As a matter of fact, the preaching of the gospel to the Gentiles may serve as a means of provoking the Jews to jealousy so that they will turn to God and be saved (Romans 11:14).

Simply put, God knows best how *and* when to mercy some and harden others (Romans 9:18). Again, as has already been stated, Romans 9:18 does not imply God's unconditional choice of some to heaven and some to hell; instead, "the hardening Paul speaks of is specific to the Jews, not all unbelievers, it is temporary, not permanent, and it is for the maximizing of salvation for all, not the display of God's justice."[137] That's why Austin Fischer can confidently affirm: "Romans 9 is one gnarly, aggressive text; however, it's aggressiveness is rooted in its mercy, not its narrowness. Romans 9 has teeth, but they're for saving, not damning."[138] God is sovereign and can have mercy on some, while he hardens others, but his purpose in both is so that "he might have mercy upon all" (Romans 11:32). It is no wonder, then, that Paul concluded Romans 9-11 with doxology: "O the depth of the riches both of the wisdom and knowledge of God! How unsearchable are his judgments, and his ways past finding out!" (Romans 11:33).

Paul, now, anticipates an objection raised to him as a result of his previous statements about God's right to have mercy. He

---

[135] Hankins, "Romans 9 and the Calvinist Doctrine of Reprobation," 71.
[136] Shank, *Elect in the Son*, 118.
[137] Hankins, "Romans 9 and the Calvinist Doctrine of Reprobation," 71.
[138] Fischer, *Young, Restless, No Longer Reformed*, 99.

predicts that his objector will ask, "Why doth he *yet* find fault? For who hath resisted his will?" This seems to be a natural question to the argument Paul has developed. If God can show mercy to the nation of Israel, while hardening Pharaoh, why does he still blame people for their actions since people cannot, apparently, resist his will? This objection, camouflaged as a question, is responded to by Paul rather abruptly: "Nay but, O man, who art thou that repliest against God?" Paul's question "demonstrates the stupidity of such a misrepresentation. How could the man reply against God if, as he [the critic] supposed, he could not resist God's will?"[139] The fact that the critic was replying against God undermines his entire objection, since he himself was resisting God's will! In any case, the notion that nobody can successfully resist the will of God is a "quite unjustifiable deduction from Paul's teaching that God's strategy is not under man's control."[140]

He, then, launches into an explanation of what God has done and is doing by offering an analogy of a potter and the clay:

> Shall the thing formed say to him that formed it,
> Why hast thou made me thus? Hath not the potter
> power over the clay, of the same lump to make one
> vessel unto honour, and another unto dishonour?
> What if God, willing to shew his wrath, and to make
> his power known, endured with much longsuffering
> the vessels of wrath fitted to destruction: and that
> he might make known the riches of his glory on the
> vessels of mercy, which he had afore prepared unto
> glory, even us, whom he hath called, not of the Jews
> only, but also of the Gentiles? (Romans 9:20b-24).

To many minds, the image of a potter with his clay brings to mind an idea of God that resembles an arbitrary despot who does with each individual creature as he deems best. However, as Marston

---

[139] Marston and Forster, *God's Strategy in Human History*, 72.
[140] Ibid., 71.

and Forster observe, "The fatalistic image brought to our western minds by this metaphor of the potter is almost the reverse of what would occur to a Hebrew mind knowing the background of the Old Testament."[141] Marston and Forster's contention is confirmed by examining how this metaphor was employed in the Old Testament. The book of Jeremiah records that the word of the Lord came to Jeremiah, instructing him to "arise, and go down to the potter's house, and there I will cause thee to hear my words" (Jeremiah 18:2). The prophet Jeremiah complied, went down to the potter's house, and watched the potter at his craft. He saw the potter take a vessel that was marred and make it good in his eyes. Notice carefully what the word of the Lord informed him after he witnessed this object lesson:

> O house of Israel, cannot I do with you as this potter? saith the Lord. Behold, as the clay is in the potter's hand, so are ye in mine hand, O house of Israel. At what instant I shall speak concerning a nation, and concerning a kingdom, to pluck up, and to pull down, and to destroy it; if that nation, against whom I have pronounced, turn from their evil, I will repent of the evil that I thought to do unto them. And at what instant I shall speak concerning a nation, and concerning a kingdom, to build and to plant it; if it do evil in my sight, that it obey not my voice, then I will repent of the good, wherewith I said I would benefit them (Jeremiah 18:6-10).

The Lord asks the nation of Israel, "Cannot I do with you as this potter?" His following comments indicate that this should not be interpreted in a fatalistic fashion, as if Israel is literally as lifeless as clay. On the contrary, if he promises to destroy a nation because of its wickedness, but that nation repents of its evil, he will relent concerning this disaster he had planned to do to it. Moreover, if God

---

[141] Ibid., 73.

announces that he is going to bless a nation, but that nation commits evil in his sight and does not obey his voice, then the Lord will not do the good he had planned to do for this nation. Clearly, then, the Lord's action as a potter is, in some manner, "depending on their own moral response."[142] Lennox notes, "The action of the potter is not capricious- the clay is living and what the potter does with it is in part dependent on its response to him."[143] N. T. Wright explains the purpose of the potter and clay analogy:

> The image of potter and clay was not designed to speak in general terms about human beings as lifeless lumps of clay, over against God as the only living, thinking being; it was designed to speak very specifically about God's purpose in choosing and calling Israel and about what would happen if Israel, like a lump of clay, failed to respond to the gentle moulding of his hands.[144]

Again, throughout this chapter, Paul has been discussing the problem of Israel's rejection of Jesus as the Messiah. He has been stressing God's sovereign right to have mercy on whomever he desires and to harden whomever he desires (Romans 9:18). He now offers the analogy of the potter and clay to emphasize that God can make, from the same lump, one vessel of honor and another of dishonor. He contends that God can shape the nation of Israel however he sees fit, in order to advance his worldwide purposes of demonstrating mercy upon all people, even if this requires a portion of the Jewish people to be vessels of dishonor. As Eric Hankins writes, "God has the right to change the destiny of Jews if they refuse to believe the gospel. Even though they have been shaped for blessing as God's people, because they reject the gospel, they are now being shaped for wrath."[145]

---

[142] Ibid.

[143] Lennox, *Determined to Believe?*, 270.

[144] Qtd in ibid.

[145] Hankins, "Romans 9 and the Calvinist Doctrine of Reprobation," 71.

It is significant how Paul contrasts the "vessels of wrath fitted to destruction" and the "vessels of mercy, which *he* had afore prepared unto glory" (Romans 9:23). Notice that Paul does *not* say that *God* prepared these vessels for destruction. Instead, they are simply "fitted to destruction." According to Vine's, the verb "fitted," as used in Romans 9:22, is in the middle voice, which "signifies that those referred to 'fitted' themselves for destruction."[146] Glen Shellrude agrees that Vine's interpretation is plausible and suggests that "the participle should be taken as a middle and implies that unbelieving Israel has prepared itself for destruction through its unbelief."[147] Thus, God endured with longsuffering these vessels of wrath who had fitted themselves for destruction. Furthermore, it is possible for vessels of wrath to become vessels of mercy. Paul describes believers as those who "were by nature the children of wrath" (Ephesians 2:3) but are now children of God by grace through faith. If Romans 9:22 meant that God had unconditionally reprobated a good portion of humanity, then it would literally be impossible for any vessel of wrath to become a vessel of mercy.

Paul's emphasis, then, is that God the potter has the sovereign prerogative to shape Israel as he sees fit. He can make one portion of Israel to be vessels that bring no honor. Those who rejected the Messiah and have fitted themselves for destruction comprise this group. Unless they repent, they will perish. However, God, in his wisdom, has shaped them for a specific task. In their rebellion, they will be used by God as a means of spreading the gospel to the gentiles. Nevertheless, individual Israelites, like the apostle Paul, can turn to the Lord and become reshaped by God into vessels of mercy. Again, the purpose of God behind shaping some to honor and others to dishonor is not to eternally save some and to eternally damn others, but to show mercy to the whole world (Romans 11:32).

---

[146] W. E. Vine, *Vine's Complete Expository Dictionary of Old and New Testament Words* (Nashville: Thomas Nelson Publishers, 1996), 241.

[147] Shellrude, "The freedom of God in mercy and judgment: a libertarian reading of Romans 9:6-29," 315.

PART 2

The Theological Problems of Calvinism

CHAPTER 4

Did Christ die
for everyone?

Many Christians would quickly affirm that Jesus Christ died for the sins of the whole world. Without the blinding presuppositions of Calvinism, most believers in Christ are not reluctant to tell everyone that "God loves you, and Christ died for you." In this book, we have attempted to point out the biblical, theological, and practical problems of Calvinism. One of the key tenets of Calvinism, especially five-point Calvinism, is that Christ died only for the elect. He did not die for everyone. This belief is known as limited atonement, definite atonement, or particular redemption. Not all Calvinists believe in limited atonement, but many of the young people in the recent resurgence of Reformed theology hold to this conviction, so it is necessary for it to be addressed and refuted.

Before continuing, though, we must differentiate between the intent, the extent, and the application of the atonement. These three terms, although very similar, refer to different aspects of the atonement. Erroneous doctrine often arises when their differences are not recognized and observed. In his recent masterpiece *The*

Extent of the Atonement, David Allen does a great job of highlighting the differences between these closely related terms:[148]

- The intent of the atonement answers the question, "What was Christ's saving *purpose* in providing an atonement?" The answer is that Christ died for all people *equally* to make salvation possible for all people, as he equally desires all to be saved, as well as secure the salvation of those who do believe.
- The extent of the atonement answers the question, "For whose sins was Christ punished?" The answer is that Jesus died for the sins of all humanity.
- The application of the atonement answers the question, "When is the atonement applied to the sinner?" The answer is that it is applied the moment the sinner exercises faith in Christ.

In this chapter, we will limit our discussion to the *extent* of the atonement. God truly loves all people and desires their salvation, and Christ died for all people, so that anyone can be saved by trusting in the person and work of Jesus Christ. However, just because Jesus has provided salvation for all of mankind does not mean that everyone will be saved. The atonement does not benefit anyone who continues to reject it. The reason why everyone will not be saved is *not* because God does not want everyone to be saved or because Christ did not die for everyone, but because many will refuse to accept the gift of salvation provided for them. Esteemed professor Paul Copan is exactly right, "The only obstacle to universal salvation is human free will and its resistance to God's loving initiative."[149]

---

[148] Allen, *The Extent of the Atonement,* xix-xx. I am quoting extensively from Allen's work in this section. I have adjusted some quotes as needed.

[149] Chad Meister and James K. Dew Jr, *God and Evil* (Downers Grove, IL: InterVarsity Press, 2013), 136.

Historical considerations

The first thing to consider about the extent of the atonement is what the church has believed throughout its history. If no Christian theologian for the first several centuries of church history taught a particular doctrine, then that particular doctrine is probably fallacious and should be rejected. The Scriptures are our supreme authority for faith, life, and practice. Nevertheless, studying church history can serve to protect us from our cultural blind spots and from falling into modern misconceptions. What is especially interesting, in relation to limited atonement, is the observation of David Allen: "The first person in church history who explicitly held belief in limited atonement was Gottschalk of Orbais (AD 804-869)."[150] That is a pretty staggering historical fact that should not be brushed aside without due consideration. This does not necessarily mean that limited atonement is wrong, but it is significant that nobody advocated a restricted view of the extent of Christ's death until the ninth century. Noteworthy also is the fact that "Gottschalk and his extreme views were condemned by three French councils."[151]

Now, if limited atonement is the biblical position, as Reformed theologians contend, why did the early church unitedly reject it? Why would God have allowed the false belief of Christ's dying for everyone to be not only the majority view but also the unanimous perspective of the church? Questions of this nature are often met with silence or answered by appeal to mystery. However, to a non-Calvinist, these responses are seen as cowardly dodges.

A brief look through the writings of the early church fathers confirms Allen's statement that Gottschalk is "the first person to argue explicitly for limited atonement in church history."[152] As he

---

[150] David L. Allen and Steve W. Lemke, *Whosoever Will* (Nashville, TN: B&H Academic, 2010), 68.

[151] Allen, *The Extent of the Atonement*, 26.

[152] Ibid., 24

affirms elsewhere, "In the patristic[153] era, it is clear from the writings of the Fathers that they understood the Scriptures to affirm that Christ's death satisfied for the sins of all mankind, but only those who believe will receive the benefits of Christ's death."[154] An example of this belief in universal atonement[155] is Eusebius (c. AD 275-339), who declared, "It was needful that the Lamb of God should be offered for the other lambs whose nature He assumed, even for the whole human race."[156] Eusebius's affirmation that Christ offered himself "for the whole human race" is consistent with Ambrose (AD 338-397):

> Christ suffered for all, rose again for all. But if anyone does not believe in Christ, he deprives himself of that general benefit ... Christ came for the salvation of all, inasmuch as He brought a remedy by which all might escape, although there are many who ... are unwilling to be healed.[157]

Eusebius and Ambrose are not alone amongst the early church fathers in this conviction that Christ died for everyone.[158] This persuasion about the universal extent of the atonement continued, in large part, as the predominant view of the church until the generation after the Reformers. Amazingly, even Martin Luther, the

---

[153] Patristic is used in reference to the early church fathers. The patristic era would be the time of these great Christian theologians.

[154] Ibid., 3.

[155] Universal atonement is the belief that Christ died for everyone, in contrast to limited atonement. Universal atonement should be differentiated with universal salvation. Although Christ has died for everyone, not everyone will be saved, because many refuse to accept the free gift of salvation.

[156] Qtd in ibid., 8.

[157] Qtd in ibid., 12.

[158] I would highly recommend Allen's *The Extent of the Atonement* (Nashville, TN: B&H Academic, 2016) for further study of this important topic. His book is dedicated to what theologians throughout the history of the church have written about the extent of the atonement.

man whose courageous efforts sparked the Protestant Reformation, did not believe in a limited atonement. He wrote, "Christ has taken away not only the sins of some men but your sins and those of the whole world. The offering was for the sins of the whole world, even though the whole world does not believe."[159] In a sermon on John 1:29, Luther proclaimed:

> You may say: "Who knows whether Christ also bore my sin? I have no doubt that He bore the sin of St. Peter, St. Paul, and other saints; these were pious people." ... Don't you hear what St. John says in our text: "This is the Lamb of God, who takes away the sin of the world"? And you cannot deny that you are also a part of this world, for you were born of man and woman. You are not a cow or a pig. It follows that your sins must be included, as well as the sins of St. Peter or St. Paul ... Don't you hear? There is nothing missing from the Lamb. He bears all the sins of the world from its inception; this implies that He also bears yours, and offers you grace.[160]

Martin Luther wasn't the only Reformer to suggest that Christ died for everyone; even John Calvin, the French Reformer who is generally credited with systematizing the doctrines that later become known as Calvinism, might not have subscribed to the theory of limited atonement. In recent years, there has been heated debate over the question of whether John Calvin affirmed limited atonement. Modern Calvinists often try to defend Calvin by asserting that although he never strictly taught that Christ died only for the elect, limited atonement is more consistent with the rest of his theology. On the other hand, non-Calvinist theologians argue that there is no way to reconcile Calvin's comments about the extent of Christ's

---

[159] Qtd in Allen, *The Extent of the Atonement*, 36.
[160] Qtd in ibid., 36,37.

death with a limited atonement. Although a statement like "Christ died for every single individual" is absent from his commentaries and sermons, Calvin does make statements that "nobody *would say* who believed in limited atonement."[161] Kevin Kennedy, in an article entitled "Was Calvin a 'Calvinist'?" in the book *Whosoever Will*, rightly points out:

> If Calvin did profess limited atonement, one would not expect to find him intentionally universalizing scriptural passages that theologians from the later Reformed tradition claim are, from a simple reading of the text, clearly teaching that Christ died only for the elect. Furthermore, if Calvin truly believed that Christ died only for the elect, then one would not expect to find Calvin claiming that unbelievers who reject the gospel are rejecting an actual provision that Christ made for them on the cross. Nor would one expect Calvin, were he a proponent of limited atonement, to fail to refute bold claims that Christ died for all of humanity when he was engaged in polemical arguments with Roman Catholics and others.[162]

The following quotations are pulled from Calvin's writings by Allen in *The Extent of the Atonement*[163] to support the contention that John Calvin did not believe in limited atonement:

> Paul makes grace common to all men, not because it in fact extends to all, but because it is offered to all. Although Christ suffered for the sins of the world, and is *offered by the goodness of God without distinction to all men*, yet not all receive him.

---

[161] Olson, *Against Calvinism*, 146. Italics his.
[162] Allen and Lemke, *Whosoever Will*, 195.
[163] These quotations are found on pp. 48-96. Italics mine.

Seeing that men are created in the image of God and that *their souls have been redeemed by the blood of Jesus Christ*, we must try in every way available to us to draw them to the knowledge of the gospel.

"Which is shed for many." By the word "many" [Paul] means not a part of the world only, but *the whole human race.*

I testify and declare that as a suppliant I humbly implore of him to grant me to be so washed and purified by the blood of that sovereign Redeemer, *shed for the sins of the human race*, that I may be permitted to stand before his tribunal in the image of the Redeemer himself.

It was to small purpose for us that Jesus Christ had redeemed us from everlasting death, and he shed his blood to reconcile us to God, unless we were certified of this benefit, and it were told us, and God should call us to enter into possession of this salvation, and to enjoy this price which was thus paid for us. As for example, *behold the Turks, which cast away the grace which was purchased for all the world by Jesus Christ.*

The hour was approaching in which our Lord Jesus would have to *suffer for the redemption of mankind.*

God, to render the wicked all the more inexcusable, willed that Jesus Christ in His death be declared sovereign King of *all creatures.*

[Paul] says that this redemption was procured through the blood of Christ, for by the sacrifice of his death *all the sins of the world* were expiated.

One more example should be sufficient for establishing that the view that Christ did not die for the sins of the entire human race is an anomaly in church history. Millard Erickson is a modern theologian who wrote a highly influential book on theology entitled *Christian Theology*.[164] In this work of systematic theology, Erickson identifies his theology as "mild Calvinism."[165] However, even though he upholds many of the doctrines of five-point Calvinism, he rejects limited atonement. He writes:

> It does not follow from a statement that Christ died for his church, for his sheep, that he did not die for anyone else, unless, of course, the passage specifically states that it was *only* for them that he died ... Certainly if Christ died for the whole, there is no problem in asserting that he died for a specific part of the whole. To insist that those passages that focus on his dying for his people require the understanding that he died only for them and not for any others contradicts the universal passages. We conclude that the hypothesis of universal atonement is able to account for a larger segment of the biblical witness with less distortion than is the hypothesis of limited atonement.[166]

This historical survey across church history has not been comprehensive, but it has confirmed an unmistakable truth. The vast majority of Christian theologians, including those who embrace what is known as Calvinism, affirm either explicitly or implicitly that Jesus Christ died for everyone. Again, while you cannot determine truth by counting noses, it is highly significant that Martin Luther and John Calvin were not ardent advocates of limited atonement.

---

[164] Millard J. Erickson, *Christian Theology- 3rd ed* (Grand Rapids, MI: BakerAcademic, 2013).

[165] Ibid., 394.

[166] Ibid., 760-761.

This should cause every Calvinist at least a moment's hesitation. Those who hold to limited atonement are more "Calvinistic" than the name bearer of the theological system they embrace.

Biblical considerations

The most important part to establishing doctrine is to believe what the Bible teaches. Historical surveys through church history can prove useful, but for anyone who upholds the authority of the Scriptures, the Bible is the final arbiter of biblical truth. If the word of God is explicit about anything, it is explicit about the fact that Jesus Christ died for everyone. Several passages in the New Testament confirm this position.

One of the clearest texts that demonstrates the universality of the extent of Christ's atonement can be found in 1 John 2:2. The Apostle John writes, "He is the propitiation for our sins: and not for ours only, but also for the sins of *the whole world.*" A careful investigation of this passage, along with the rest of John's writings, would support Robert Picirilli's contention that John's meaning in 1 John 2:2 is "that believers, even when discussing the benefits of Christ's atoning death for themselves, must remember that He also died for the whole world, including the lost."[167]

John only uses the phrase "the whole world" one more time in 1 John. In 1 John 5:19, he notes, "And we know that we are of God, and *the whole world* lieth in wickedness." Clearly, in this verse, John contrasts the believers with the rest of the world who lie in their iniquities and transgressions. Comparing 1 John 5:19, then, with 1 John 2:2 yields the correct interpretation. Just as the whole world lies in wickedness, so also Christ has died for the whole world. If John's use of the phrase "the whole world" in 1 John 5:19 includes the rest of humanity in contrast to those who are believing, then his use of the same phrase should include the same individuals.

---

[167] Robert Picirilli, *Grace, Faith, Free Will* (Nashville, TN: Randall House, 2002), 132.

Another unambiguous passage used to strengthen the case for the universal extent of the atonement is found in Paul's first letter to Timothy. Paul instructs Timothy that "there is one God, and one mediator between God and men, the man Christ Jesus; who gave himself a ransom for all, to be testified in due time" (1 Timothy 2:5,6). To show that a universal atonement is intended by Paul, here are the preceding verses:

> I exhort therefore, that, first of all, supplications, prayers, intercessions, and giving of thanks, be made for all men; for kings, and for all that are in authority; that we may lead a quiet and peaceable life in all godliness and honesty. For this is good and acceptable in the sight of God our Saviour; who will have all men to be saved, and to come unto the knowledge of the truth (1 Timothy 2:1-4).

William Sailer's observation is correct: "The context demands a universal application."[168] Paul begins the chapter by encouraging prayers to be made for all, which is based on God's earnest desire for all men to be saved. This is the foundation for the redemptive work of Jesus Christ, who serves as the only mediator between sinful people and a holy God and who offered himself as a ransom for all men. Calvinists' efforts to restrict the scope of this passage is driven more by a desire to protect a theological system than to exegete the Scriptures.

In order to guard their fallacious doctrine, Calvinists engage in radical reinterpretations of the clear meaning of the Bible. A question, then, needs to be asked: How else could God have communicated this in a more forceful and straightforward manner than he did throughout the pages of Scripture? If Christ did in fact die for everyone, how could the Scriptures state this any more clearly? After all, Jesus Christ died for "the whole world" (1 John

---

[168] William Sailer, "The Nature and Extent of the Atonement- A Wesleyan View," *Bulletin of the Evangelical Theological Society* 10 (1967): 193.

2:2); he gave himself for "all" (1 Timothy 2:6); and he "tasted death for every man" (Hebrews 2:9). For anyone to deny that the extent of the atonement is universal, he needs to ask himself why God chose to inspire the Scriptures in a way that seems to clearly imply the universal extent of Christ's death. Perhaps, though, the Calvinist's *a priori* assumptions prevent the Scriptures from teaching that Christ died for everyone. If limited atonement is true, then God did a very poor job of communicating that through his word.

Not only are there several passages that highlight the universal extent of Christ's death, but there are also different places in the New Testament that indicate that "Christ died for some who may be lost."[169] Roger Olson, in his book *Against Calvinism*, marshals 1 Corinthians 8:11 as a verse that "unequivocally contradicts" the doctrine of limited atonement.[170] In this passage, Paul is urging those strong in the faith to avoid using their Christian freedom to eat meat in a pagan temple so that someone weak in the faith does not stumble. Paul's warning is serious, "And through thy knowledge shall the weak brother perish, *for whom Christ died?*" (1 Corinthians 8:11). Olson's comment is fitting: "If limited atonement is true, Paul's warning is an empty threat because it cannot happen. A person for whom Christ died cannot be destroyed."[171] First Corinthians 8:11 demands that Christ died for everyone. It is possible that our behavior as Christians could cause some weaker believers, people that Christ died for, to stumble and perish eternally in hell.

Paul isn't the only New Testament author to indicate that people purchased by Christ's death will reject this provision. In his second epistle, Peter signifies that there were false teachers who were denying the Lord who bought them. Listen to what he says: "But there were false prophets also among the people, even as there shall be false teachers among you, who privily shall bring in damnable heresies, *even denying the Lord that bought them,* and bring upon themselves swift destruction" (2 Peter 2:1). Calvinists engage in exegetical gymnastics

---

[169] Ibid., 191.

[170] Olson, *Against Calvinism*, 147.

[171] Ibid.

to make this simple statement harmonize with their theological system. However, the Bible should determine our theology, not the other way around.

One more example from the Scriptures should suffice in demonstrating that some people for whom Christ died will be lost and go to hell. Again, the reason why it is important to illustrate this is because Calvinists believe that everyone Christ died for (the elect) will be saved. According to Calvinism, Christ died only for those who were chosen in eternity past, and his death secures their salvation. Therefore, if the word of God teaches that people for whom Christ died will not be saved, then the doctrine of limited atonement is proven to be unscriptural.

Let me ask you a question: Did Jesus die for Judas? If Jesus died for Judas, then he died for someone who died unsaved. Judas betrayed the Lord for thirty silver coins (Matthew 26:14-16). After seeing that Jesus was condemned, regret filled his heart, and he returned to the chief priests and elders to give them back the silver coins. They did not accept his apology, so he threw the money into the temple, ran away, and hanged himself (Matthew 27:1-5). Clearly, Judas had forsaken Christ, but did Christ die for Judas? Luke's account of the Last Supper indicates that Jesus shed his blood for Judas: "This cup is the new testament in my blood, which is shed for *you*. But, behold, the hand of him that betrayeth me is with me on the table" (Luke 22:20,21). Jesus says that his blood is "shed for you" and then informs his apostles that the one who would betray him was at the table. A further indication that Judas was at the table comes earlier in this same chapter: "And when the hour was come, he sat down, and the *twelve apostles* with him" (Luke 22:14). Without a doubt, Judas was sitting at the table during the Last Supper when Jesus said that his blood was poured out for "you." In summary, here is the evidence that Jesus died for Judas:

1. Jesus tells his twelve apostles, including Judas, that he would shed his blood for them.

2. Judas betrays Jesus, hangs himself, and is thus consigned to eternal damnation.

3. Therefore, Jesus died for someone (Judas) who would not be saved.

Practical Considerations

There are serious implications to rejecting universal atonement. For starters, denying that Christ died for everyone leads also to a "diminishing of God's universal saving will."[172] It is contradictory to assert that God truly desires the salvation of all people if Christ has not also died for all people. The Scriptures are emphatic that God desires everyone to be saved (1 Timothy 2:4); he is "not willing that any should perish, but that all should come to repentance" (2 Peter 3:9); and he does not have "pleasure in the death of the wicked" (Ezekiel 33:11). The attempts of Calvinists to reconcile the abundant testimony of God's universal saving will with their theological system are bankrupt and vivid illustrations of the contradictions that Calvinism creates. The truth is this: because God genuinely longs for everyone to be saved, Christ has died for everyone, and anyone can be saved by repenting of their sins and believing the gospel.

Furthermore, limited atonement impacts the sincere offer of the gospel. As believers, we are commanded to proclaim the good news of Jesus Christ around the world, to call men and women to repentance, and to preach reconciliation. However, belief that Christ did not die for all people erodes the foundation of the well-meant offer. Furthermore, Paul informs us that when we spread the gospel, God makes his appeal through us: "Now then we are ambassadors for Christ, as though God did beseech you by us: we pray you in Christ's stead, be ye reconciled to God" (2 Corinthians 5:20). In this passage, God implores people through his ambassadors to be reconciled. He is offering salvation through this appeal. David Allen's inquiry is

---

[172] Allen, *The Extent of the Atonement*, 785.

precise: "How can he do this according to limited atonement since there is no provision for the salvation of the non-elect in the death of Christ?"[173]

Imagine yourself standing in front of a crowd of people in a third-world country. You have been invited to share the gospel of Jesus Christ with people who have never heard the name of Jesus. As you near the end of your sermon, you are wanting to confront these precious souls with the need to follow Christ. You explain the sinfulness of man and how every person is in need of a Savior. Then, you make the appeal, "Christ died for *you!*" Let's pause for a second: Could a Calvinist honestly make this statement? I don't think so. It would be untrue to his theology to tell the audience that Christ died for them since there might be people who are non-elect. That's why Roger Olson wrote with audacity, "*If* you believe that there may be some in your audience who cannot be saved because Christ made no provision for their salvation, you *cannot in all honesty* preach that all may come to Christ through repentance and faith because Christ died for them."[174]

Many Calvinists will typically respond to this by saying that they don't know who the elect are and that they just preach and let God save his people. In order to accomplish this task of preaching to all people even though Christ did not die for all people, they often use vague statements that camouflage their doctrine of limited atonement. A recent example of this duplicity is Greg Gilbert's *What Is the Gospel?*[175] Many Christians unfamiliar with the jargon of Calvinism would not suspect that the author of this book supports limited atonement. Perhaps, the aim of the author is to disguise this distasteful doctrine. Whatever the reason, the use of unclear, ambiguous phrases about the extent of the atonement has proven to be successful in the recent resurgence of Reformed theology. It is essential, then, to be aware of this maneuver so that you are not deceived by what someone actually believes.

---

[173] Ibid., 786.

[174] Olson, *Against Calvinism*, 151.

[175] Greg Gilbert, *What Is the Gospel?* (Wheaton, IL: Crossway, 2010).

So, what are some examples of this disguise? Two phrases are especially common in Calvinistic circles. With some minor wording changes, those phrases are "Christ died for *sinners*" or "Christ died to save *his people*." The use of these expressions in Calvinists' literature is prevalent, and Gilbert's book is a conspicuous representation. He writes, "King Jesus came not only to inaugurate the kingdom of God, but also *to bring sinners* into it by dying in their place and for their sin, taking their punishment on himself and securing forgiveness for them ..."[176] Later on, he continues:

> When Jesus died, it was not the punishment for his own sins that he endured. (He didn't have any!) It was the punishment for *his people's sins!* As he hung on the cross at Calvary, Jesus all the horrible weight of *the sin of God's people.* All their rebellion, all their disobedience, all their sin fell on his shoulders.[177]

Jesus died for sinners and his people? What's the big deal with that? Anyone who reads the Bible will come to these conclusions. The problem is that "his people" and "sinners" are code words for the elect. Thus, when Gilbert writes that Jesus was punished "for his people's sins," what he means is that Jesus was *only* punished for the sins of those chosen for salvation by God in eternity past. For a Calvinist, such as Gilbert, saying that Christ died for sinners is just another way of expressing the doctrine of limited atonement. Again, those foreign to Calvinism would probably not detect the subtle usage of these words, but it is an unmistakable fact:

> When high Calvinists use the terminology "Christ died for sinners," the term "sinners" becomes something of a code word for "the elect only." In order to be consistent with their theology, Calvinists

---

[176] Ibid., 64. Italics mine.

[177] Ibid., 67. Italics mine.

must resort to the deliberately vague statement "Christ died for sinners."[178]

Not only is this approach dishonest, but Calvinists also miss the point when they assert that because they do not know who the elect are, they preach to everyone. Again, David Allen is helpful in pointing out the problematic position of a preacher who believes in limited atonement:

> The issue is not that we don't know who the elect are ... The issue is we are offering something to all people, including those who turn out to be non-elect, that indeed does not exist for all to whom the offer is made. An offer made to all sinners entails contradiction as the preacher knows that the satisfaction for sins by Christ on the cross was not made for all to whom the gospel comes, but he pretends and speaks as if there is a legitimate offer to all to whom the gospel is preached.[179]

Amazingly, in the Calvinistic system, the reprobate are condemned eternally for not receiving an atonement that did not exist for them. Or, as William Sailer put it, "If God has not provided [atonement] for all, then the non-elect are condemned for refusing to believe a lie!"[180] This explains why limited atonement hinders evangelism, missions, and preaching. Obviously, many Calvinists have been tremendous missionaries and evangelists that have led souls to Christ through the preaching of the cross, but it does seem evident that a denial of Christ's universal atonement would negatively

---

[178] Allen, *The Extent of the Atonement*, 786.

[179] Ibid., 774.

[180] Sailer, "The Nature and Extent of the Atonement- A Wesleyan View," 195.

influence evangelism. Roger Olson rightly asks, "How can belief in limited atonement *not* hinder evangelism?"[181]

Arguments used by Calvinists

It might be useful, now, to address the different reasons employed by Calvinists to construct a defense of limited atonement. One of the most frequent arguments advanced by the Calvinist is constructed from John 17:9, "I pray for them: I pray not for the world, but for them which thou hast given me; for they are thine." Calvinists use this verse to support their teaching of limited atonement. Although it does not address the question of whom Christ died for, it does limit the scope of his praying. In this verse, Jesus specifically states that he doesn't pray for the world; he prays only "for them which thou hast given me," which, to a Calvinist, means the elect.

So, the typical Calvinist argument is something along the lines of what R. C. Sproul presented in his book *What is Reformed Theology?*[182] Based on John 17:9, he contended:

> Jesus intercedes here in behalf of those whom the Father has given him. It is abundantly clear that this does not include all mankind. The Father gave to Christ a *limited* number of people. They are the ones for whom Christ prays. They are also the ones for whom Christ died. Jesus does not pray for the whole world. He says that directly and clearly. He prays specifically for the ones given to him, the elect.[183]

---

[181] Olson, *Against Calvinism*, 152.
[182] R. C. Sproul, *What Is Reformed Theology?* (Grand Rapids, MI: Baker Books, 1997).
[183] Ibid., 175.

As Sproul asked elsewhere, "Did Christ die for those for whom he would not pray?"[184] A brief look at his reasoning might seem persuasive, but a couple of remarks can be made in response to this argument. First, does it logically follow that if Christ doesn't pray for someone, then he couldn't have died for them? As seen above, the Scriptures teach that Christ died for the sins of the whole world (1 John 2:2) and was a ransom for all (1 Timothy 2:6). To begin with John 17:9 and infer that this prayer limits the extent of the atonement is to reveal one's biased presuppositions.

Second, this explanation fails to consider the rest of the passage. It's honestly baffling when Calvinists employ this argument because Jesus proceeds, in the very same prayer, to pray for those who will believe through the word of the disciples (John 17:20) and for the world (John 17:21,23). The only rational justification for this egregious oversight is that the Calvinist has engaged in proof-texting, which caused him to take John 17:9 out of context to the neglect of the remainder of the paragraph.

Why, then, does Jesus pray only for those who have been given to him in John 17:9? This expression of people being given to Jesus is unique to the Gospel of John and refers to his disciples while he was "down from heaven" (John 6:38). They were the Father's people (John 17:6), having listened to and learned from him (John 6:45). This faithful Jewish remnant had been given to Jesus. He then proceeded to give them the message he was sent to deliver (John 17:8). Jesus prays a special prayer for them because they are about to be sent into the world (John 17:18) to proclaim the gospel and make disciples of all nations. This is an important task that requires extreme commitment in the face of adversity, so he prays for their protection from the evil one (John 17:15) and for their sanctification (John 17:17).

How else do advocates of limited atonement protect their historically, biblically, and practically tenuous stance on the extent of the atonement? To support their perspective, Calvinists often appeal to the passages in Scriptures that speak of Christ dying

---

[184] Sproul, *Chosen by God*, 206.

for a limited number of people. For example, Jesus himself stated, "I am the good shepherd: the good shepherd giveth his life for the sheep ... I lay down my life for the sheep" (John 10:11,15). Furthermore, Paul encourages husbands to love their wives "as Christ also loved the church and gave himself for it" (Ephesians 5:25). So, advocates of limited atonement reason that Christ died only for believers. He did not die for everyone; instead, he died only for those unconditionally chosen by God for salvation before the foundations of the world.

There are a number of flaws with this reasoning. For starters, as Charles Finney noted, this is the same logic that Unitarians use to deny the deity of Christ. In order to substantiate their position, Unitarians will emphasize verses that speak about the humanity of Christ and infer that because Christ was a man, he couldn't have also been God.[185] Likewise, limited atonement advocates highlight the verses that state that Christ died for the church, the elect, or the sheep and reason that he did not die for anyone else.

However, just because Christ died for a particular group of people does not logically negate the fact that he died for the sins of the whole world. If Christ died for the whole world, then, necessarily, he also died for the sins of any particular group of people. Adam Harwood maintains, "Affirming that Christ died for all is not a denial that Christ died for some (the sheep, the elect, and the church of God). Rather, affirming that Christ died for all is a denial that Christ died *only* for some."[186] No verse in the entire Bible says that Christ died *only* for the elect. Those who promote limited atonement insert this *a priori* assumption into these passages and explain the universal passages (1 John 2:2; 1 Timothy 2:6) in a limited fashion. Again, believing that Christ died for the whole world is not contradicted by saying that he also died for a group in the whole world.

---

[185] Charles Finney, *Finney's Systematic Theology* (Minneapolis, MN: Bethany House Publishers, 1994), 228.

[186] Adam Harwood, "Is the Gospel for All People or Only Some People?" *JBTM* 11 (2014): 25. Italics mine.

A simple analogy might help you comprehend the faulty logic of the Calvinist, which commits "the negative inference fallacy."[187] Suppose that a businessman named Jones provides lunch for an entire Christian school. Because of the size of the cafeteria, each class eats by itself, so third graders do not eat with fifth graders and seventh graders do not eat with tenth graders. You have two children in the school: Billy, who is in second grade, and Suzy, who is in eighth grade. On the way home from school, Suzy comments that Jones had provided lunch for her class. Now, consider this question: Does the fact that Jones provided lunch for Suzy's class mean that he did not provide lunch for Billy's class? Of course not! However, if you employed the logic that Calvinists use in arguing for the extent of the atonement, you might be forced to conclude that Jones provided lunch *only* for Suzy's class.

Returning to the extent of the atonement, that Christ died for the church does not mean that Christ died *only* for the church. Paul, for example, wrote that Christ "loved me, and gave himself for me" (Galatians 2:20). Is it reasonable to conclude from Paul's joyous statement that Christ died only for Paul? Absolutely not! Similarly, it is just as absurd to infer that because Christ died for a particular group of people, he did not die for the whole world.

A third and final prevalent argument for limited atonement can be summarized by a question asked by R. C. Sproul: "Is Christ a real Savior or merely a 'potential' Savior?"[188] Calvinists often contend that Christ did not come to make salvation possible; instead, he came to actually save. In his book *For Calvinism*, Michael Horton insists that "Scripture nowhere teaches that Christ came into the world to make salvation possible, much less that it becomes actual because of faith in Christ."[189] For a Calvinist, to state that Christ died to provide for the potential salvation of all men is to leave open the possibility, at least theoretically, that no one would be

---

[187] Allen, *The Extent of the Atonement*, 784.

[188] Sproul, *What Is Reformed Theology?*, 164.

[189] Michael Horton, *For Calvinism* (Grand Rapids, MI: Zondervan, 2011), 92.

saved. Mark Dever, for example, uses this line of reasoning against universal atonement:

> [No] language in the New Testament refers to something potential, a mere possibility, or an option; rather, each image refers to something that actually accomplishes its end or purpose. So, for example, how can we say that God and sinners are reconciled if these "reconciled sinners" were then cast into hell? Or what kind of propitiation would it be if God's wrath was not assuaged, or what kind of redemption if the hostages were not set free? The point with all these images is that the benefit envisioned has not merely been made available; it has been secured not by the mere teaching ministry of Christ but by his death and resurrection.[190]

As can be clearly seen, the Calvinistic understanding of the atonement is that everyone for whom Christ died will be saved. Reformed writers David Steele and Curtis Thomas contend:

> Historical or main line Calvinism has consistently maintained that Christ's redeeming work was definite in design and accomplishment- that it was intended to render complete satisfaction for certain specified sinners and that it actually secured salvation for these individuals and for no one else. The salvation which Christ earned for His people includes everything involved in bringing them into a right relationship with God, including the gifts of faith and repentance. Christ did not die simply to make it possible for God to pardon sinners. Neither does God leave it up to sinners as to whether or not

---

[190] Mark Dever, *The Gospel & Personal Evangelism* (Wheaton, IL: Crossway, 2007), 38-39.

Christ's work will be effective. On the contrary, all for whom Christ sacrificed will be saved infallibly.[191]

Based, then, on this understanding of the atonement, advocates of limited atonement proceed to accuse non-Calvinists of believing in "a Christ who tried to save everybody but actually saved nobody."[192] Several comments can be made in response to this argument. First, as Jerry Walls and Joe Dongell observe, "It is a scenario that hasn't materialized. By the witness of Scripture itself, many scores of souls have believed and have received full salvation."[193] Not only do the Scriptures testify to the fact that thousands of souls were saved by believing in the gospel of Jesus Christ, but personal experience verifies the reality that Christ is still saving souls in the twenty-first century. Our doctrines should be established not through hypothetical situations but through the infallible word of God.

Furthermore, Calvinists who use this argument commit the logical fallacy of a false dilemma. In his seminal work *Elect in the Son*, Robert Shank highlights this exact mistake. He notes:

> Here is that ubiquitous theological bugbear, an assumed either ... or. Christ came to do both: to make the salvation of all men possible (which is by no means a 'merely') and to save His people from their sins. The former purpose is in order to the latter, and the fact that the atonement is universally sufficient in no way impinges on the fact that it is particularly efficient.[194]

Shank is exactly right. Christ died to potentially save all men and to actually save those who believe in him. Again, there is a difference between the extent of the atonement and the application

---

[191] Steele and Thomas, *The Five Points of Calvinism*, 39.
[192] Sproul, *Chosen by God*, 207.
[193] Walls and Dongell, *Why I Am Not a Calvinist*, 71.
[194] Shank, *Elect in the Son*, 72.

of the atonement. Calvinists have, unfortunately, confused these two separate topics. Just because Christ died for someone does not necessarily mean that this individual will be saved. In order to be saved, the atonement must be applied to his life. Shank, again, provides a concise way to summarize this difference:

> Atonement has been wrought in Christ- an objective atonement efficacious for all who believe ... An objective reconciliation has been accomplished for all mankind. Jesus "gave himself a ransom for *all*" (1 Tim. 2:6) and "by the righteousness of [Jesus] the free gift came upon *all men* unto justification of life" (Rom. 5:18) ... What has been provided must be appropriated. What is objective must become subjective.[195]

---

[195] Shank, *Life in the Son*, 26. Italics mine.

CHAPTER 5

Is God a Sovereign Tyrant?

Before addressing the subject of the sovereignty of God a few statements about the nature of God will serve as a platform to address the subject matter of the sovereignty of God. Beneficial to the discussion of this topic is a consideration of the attributes of God. Whether the attributes are categorized as moral or non-moral, related or non-related, it is mandatory that the interpretation of God's attributes be consistent with his nature. For instance, one must note God's attribute of pure actuality (God has no potential to not exist and is the uncaused Cause of all that began to exist – Genesis 1:1; Colossians 1:17). Therefore, God is a necessary Being. Furthermore, consideration must be given to God's simplicity (God cannot be divided and is an absolute unity in the Trinity – 1 Timothy 2:5). Next, God's aseity (God is eternally self-existent in and of Himself – Psalms 90:2) should be considered. Moreover, the immutability of God (God is unchanging in His nature – Hebrews 13:8) should penetrate our thinking. Finally, regardless of the doctrinal issue that may be raised, the fact remains that man must understand the sovereignty of God in light of general and scriptural revelation and spiritual manifestations of His attributes.

It is important to define the sovereignty of God before proceeding to challenge the fallacious Calvinistic teaching of divine determinism. Norman Geisler maintained "Technically, sovereignty is not an attribute of God, but rather the activity of God in relation to His universe … Sovereignty is God's right to control all things."[196] In addition, noted theologian H. C. Thiessen observed, "The sovereignty of God is not an attribute, but a prerogative of God arising out of the perfections of His nature."[197] Similarly, Merrill Unger wrote, "The supreme rulership of God is rightly held to be not an attribute of God, but a prerogative based upon the perfections of the divine Being."[198] In other words, the sovereignty of God is not a separate attribute of God, but is based in His attributes. Although some prefer to view and classify the sovereignty of God as an attribute, the argument remains the same. The sovereignty of God cannot contradict or conflict with any other attribute. Thus, as Robert Picirilli understood, "God's sovereignty means that He is absolutely free to act as He wills and in accord with His own nature. To put this another way, His actions are not 'conditioned' by any considerations other than being true to Himself."[199]

The Calvinistic doctrine of divine determinism maintains that, since God is absolutely sovereign, he predetermines and causes all decisions and actions. The fallacy of this perspective is equating absolute sovereignty with divine determinism, which results in a conflict between the sovereignty of God and human responsibility. This error will be refuted by analyzing the nature of God through His attributes and advocating the biblical position of libertarian free will. A brief examination of the fall of Adam in the Garden of Eden establishes the groundwork for the biblical and doctrinal defense of man's self-determinism. In Genesis 3, the Bible records

---

[196] Geisler, *Systematic Theology in One Volume*, 677.

[197] H. C. Thiessen, *Introductory Lectures in Systematic Theology* (Grand Rapids, MI: Wm. B. Eerdmans Publishing Company, 1977), 128.

[198] Merrill F. Unger, *Unger's Bible Dictionary* (Chicago, IL: Moody Press, 1966), 1041.

[199] Picirilli, *Grace, Faith, Free Will*, 21.

the temptation and fall of Adam and Eve. A reading of that tragic event will reveal several important truths. First, the deceptive approach Satan took to deceive Adam and Eve indicates he does not have the power to cause one to sin but possesses the power only to tempt. Second, God did not cause Adam to sin. In James 1:13, the Bible states, "Let no man say when he is tempted, I am tempted of God: for God cannot be tempted with evil, neither tempteth he any man." Neither through primary nor secondary causes will the nature of God allow Him to be the author of sin. Third, Adam had no inclination or predisposition to disobey God. Also, he was equipped with the word and counsel of God, and he was in a perfect, sinless environment. There was no causal effect to influence Adam to sin. Fourth, the potential to obey or disobey resided in the free will of Adam. Adam, himself, determined to sin. Thus, God, who is sovereign, created self-determinism.

Absolute Sovereignty vs. Arbitrary Sovereignty

Professor Gunther H. Juncker wrote a powerful article concerning the problem of theistic determinism. In the article he noted, "If determinism is true either God is evil and the author of evil *or* all talk of good and evil, of praise and blame, of moral responsibility, and of justice is meaningless and incomprehensible with reference to God."[200] God, as portrayed by theistic determinism, is a God who manifests himself through arbitrary sovereignty. Consequently, a tremendous contradiction is created between the definitions of absolute and arbitrary sovereignty. How can a good God create, sanction, or decree evil for the maximization of His glory? How can a just God judge and punish a man for doing exactly what God predestinated for him to do? Calvinism attempts to answer this apparent contradiction in the nature of God by arguing that God has two wills. God's first will is his perceptive will, which involves what

---

[200] Gunther H. Juncker, "The Dilemma of Theistic Determinism," *Journal of Baptist Theology & Ministry* 12 (2015): 15.

God wants a man to do as revealed in the Scriptures. His second will is his decretive will, meaning what will actually happen in time according to God's decree. However, this argument fails because it is contradictory. When the perceptive and decretive (which always prevails) wills conflict, the result is clearly stated by Thomas McCall: "You are guilty of doing what I told you not to do … and you are guilty of that because you did what I decreed that you would do (and could not avoid doing)."[201]

Calvinists will often reply that God directly or indirectly works through secondary causes. However, Juncker explains the shortcoming of this explanation: "In a fully determined world where the ultimate and final evil outcome was known, intended, and the only possible outcome realized, all blame resides with the one who created the world."[202] To assert that a holy, good, and just God would cause or determine evil for the greater good or his self-glorification is a blasphemous idea and a blatant assault on the nature of God. Juncker provides an excellent description of the horrific effects of divine determinism:

> Determinism is an acid that corrodes beyond recognition everything it comes into contact with. It destroys all that we ordinarily mean by causation, compulsion, free will, good and evil, justice, moral responsibility, permission, praise and blame, sovereignty, etc. Theistic determinism must be rejected if we are to make any meaningful sense of ourselves, our world, God's Word, and-most importantly-God Himself.[203]

Arbitrary (capricious, whimsical, unpredictable) sovereignty finds no place in the nature of God. Distinguished theologians from

---

[201] Thomas H. McCall, "We Believe in God's Sovereign Goodness," *Trinity Journal* 29 (2008): 240.

[202] Juncker, "The Dilemma of Theistic Determinism," 18.

[203] Ibid., 22.

a variety of denominational backgrounds soundly reject the idea of arbitrary sovereignty. John Miley wrote, "We raise no question respecting a true divine sovereignty, but discard a purely arbitrary one as utterly inconsistent with the character and the great facts of his providence ... an arbitrary sovereignty can have no other reason for its acts than its own arbitrariness."[204] Thiessen concurred, "The sovereignty of God is not exercised on the basis of arbitrary will, but on that of His wise and holy counsel."[205] Thus, the fallacious teaching of divine determinism is a picture of arbitrariness and is unthinkable and repulsive. A citation from the *Encyclopedia of Religion and Ethics* confirms this conclusion:

> A doctrine of divine sovereignty that ends, as do Augustinianism and Calvinism, in the election of the few, and the reprobation of the many has evidently started wrong-not from the Christian conception of God as revealed in Christ, but from a conception of sovereignty that in every country today which enjoys any measure of constitutional liberty would be repudiated as false.[206]

Because God is sovereign, He chose to create man with free will or self-determinism. This does not alter or affect God's divine sovereignty, remove God's grace, or allow man to save himself. What this does is bestow to man human responsibility and thus accountability for his freely chosen actions. Without libertarian free will the conclusion would be "to attribute human sinful behaviors to God (if he controls all that happens in a deterministic way)."[207] After extensively writing on the sovereignty of God, Charles Finney declared, "The idea of arbitrary sovereignty is shocking and revolting,

---

[204] Miley, *Systematic Theology – Volume II*, 222-223.

[205] Thiessen, *Introductory Lectures in Systematic Theology*, 173.

[206] James Hastings, ed., *Encyclopedia of Religion and Ethics* (New York, NY: Charles Scribner's Sons, 1921), 759.

[207] Klein, *The New Chosen People*, 269.

not only to the human heart, whether unregenerate or regenerate, but also to the human intelligence."[208] A. W. Tozer describes the relationship between God's sovereignty and human freedom:

> God's sovereignty is God's absolute freedom to do whatever He ordains to do … God created man in His own image, and in His sovereign and absolute freedom He ordained that man was to have a limited amount of freedom; and that was God's sovereign decree; that man should have some freedom. So, when man exercises his freedom, he is fulfilling the sovereignty of God, not cancelling it out.[209]

The Sovereignty of God and Moral Law

Romans 2:12-19 establishes the biblical basis for God's institution of an objective moral law which is written on the hearts of all men. Without controversy God's absolute sovereignty extends over all creation, and in relationship to mankind, it is applicable and manifested in moral order. W. T. Conner remarked, "Since man is a rational and moral being, he cannot be controlled merely by physical or mechanical law. His obedience to God must be by choice. But whether man chooses to obey or disobey, he is still under moral law. He cannot free himself from its demands."[210] In addition to the biblical revelation of a moral law, ancient historical writings centuries before the time of Christ establish the fact that all societies, no matter how large or small, maintained moral absolutes. Clearly, as C. S. Lewis advocated, "There are universal moral laws. If there were not, we would not be able to engage in moral disputes, to make moral judgments, or to discern the moral progress (or regress) of

---

[208] Finney, *Finney's Systematic Theology*, 93.

[209] Qtd in Klein, *The New Chosen People*, 298.

[210] W. T. Conner, *The Faith of the New Testament* (Nashville, TN: Broadman Press, 1940), 71.

society."[211] One may justifiably conclude with J. Daryl Charles that "human beings are morally free agents, exercising their free will … If there is no content to their decisions, then moral action-indeed, all actions, are meaningless."[212]

The awareness of an objective moral law is seen through the operation of the conscience. The existence of the conscience is undeniable yet inexplicable in its functioning. Regardless of the individual or society, there is the sense of right and wrong which guides man to the truth that he 'ought' to conduct himself in a certain way. Earl Martin contended, "Conscience, then, in its complete sense, includes a searching for the right in forming moral judgments, an allegiance to right because of this obligation of oughtness, and when the right is done, the approval of the moral person. Or vice versa in the case of wrong conduct."[213] Biblical references concerning the conscience reveal that the conscience may be good (1 Peter 2:9); evil (Hebrews 10:22); seared (1Timothy 4:2); convicted (John 8:9); and pure (1 Timothy 3:9). Although this is not an exhaustive list, enough is stated to reveal that they appropriate realization and functioning of moral law in man's free will. There must be an engraved moral and just code for man to determine what are immoral and unjust actions. This will allow the conscience to make moral choices in accord with their moral judgment.

America is a sovereign nation, but who would believe that the government has the right to confiscate one's property, arrest him and put him in prison, and allow him no rebuttal or recourse and justify such action as permissible, legal, acceptable, and moral based on sovereignty? One would rightfully declare such action is unconstitutional and totalitarian because "there is imprinted on the hearts of men a discrimination and judgment, by which they distinguish between justice and injustice, honesty and dishonesty. It is

---

[211] Qtd in Geisler, *Systematic Theology in One Volume*, 1205.

[212] J. Daryl Charles, *Retrieving the Natural Law* (Grand Rapids: Wm. B. Eerdmans, 2008), 157.

[213] Earl Martin, *Toward Understanding God* (Anderson, IN: Gospel Trumpet Company, 1942), 111.

what makes them ashamed of adultery and theft."[214] Men understand and engage in horizontal relationships based on the moral law of God. If men, who are finite, function in this relationship, how is it that God arbitrarily contradicts the moral law that he placed in their hearts? This cannot be a true characterization of God's attitude and actions. Again, as has already been discussed, "God's sovereign will and power are not arbitrary, despotic, or deterministic; his sovereignty is characterized by his justice and holiness as well as by his other attributes."[215]

The erroneous doctrine of divine determinism taught by Reformed theology and, in particular, the advocacy of unconditional election contradict both God's moral law and God's nature. According to the *Evangelical Dictionary of Theology*, "It certainly would be contradictory to divine justice to condemn people to eternal separation from God for not living according to a standard they never had and never knew."[216] Jesus reveals in Matthew 25:31-46 that man's horizontal relationships represent and are a picture of man's vertical relationship with God. If man can understand justice, goodness, human responsibility and love, how is it that God acts arbitrarily for His own self-glory? Consider Norman's Geisler's powerful observation:

> Something is not right just because God wills it; He wills it because it is right in accordance with His unchangeable nature. God's will is not arbitrary. He cannot decide tomorrow that hate is good and love is bad. His will cannot be cut loose from His immutable nature. Hence, contrary to extreme Calvinism, God cannot simply will to love some people (the elect) and provide salvation only for

---

[214] Geisler, *Systematic Theology in One Volume*, 1203.

[215] Walter A. Elwell, ed., *Evangelical Dictionary of Theology* (Grand Rapids, MI: Baker Book House, 1984), 1039.

[216] Ibid., 1204.

them. God is love (1 John 4:16) by His very nature
and cannot change.[217]

It is abundantly clear that God is the creator and giver of moral
law. Thus, the institution of libertarian free will allows man to
freely obey the moral government of God. Finney reasoned, "The
human mind necessarily assumes the freedom of the human will as
a first truth. First truths, let it be remembered, are those that are
necessarily assumed by every moral agent. They are assumed always
and necessarily by a law of the intelligence."[218] This rationally leads
to the conclusion that self-determinism is the foundational principle
in an understanding of free moral agency. Geisler's comments, again,
are terrific: "The fact that we 'ought' to do certain things implies
that we can do them. 'Ought' implies can ... In this evil world, our
freedom or self-determination involves the choice either to do good
or to do evil. Without this ability to do otherwise, we would not be
free."[219] Connected to the human mind are rational, moral, and
religious motives. Thus, the creation of and accountability to moral
law necessitates the capacity for man to be able to make necessary
moral and religious choices. Romans 2:1 validates that very truth by
declaring that all men are accountable to moral law.

In summary, to posit the idea that the 'non-elect' could never
exercise the motives that God demands of them and then hold them
accountable for their failure to meet the obligations of moral law is
atrocious. To suggest that the 'non-elect' do not have the motive,
capacity, or ability to choose Christ, the righteous Savior, and live
a holy life contradicts the understanding of moral law and the very
nature of God. Nothing but chaos, confusion, and the creation of
categories and mysteries can come from such deterministic teaching.
This is exemplified in the egregious error of total inability, where free
will is in bondage to the flesh and man cannot choose spiritual good.

---

[217] Norman L. Geisler, *Chosen But Free*, (Minneapolis, MN: Bethany House,
2010), 150.

[218] Finney, *Finney's Systematic Theology*, 307.

[219] Geisler, *Chosen But Free*, 127.

The Sovereignty of God and Aseity

God is self-existent, the uncaused Cause, a necessary Being, and changeless in His nature. It is imperative, then, that one understands the meaning and significance of God's attribute of aseity. Aseity "comes from the Latin *a,* meaning from, and *se,* meaning oneself. God is underived, necessary, nondependent existence. Understanding that God is noncontingent helps to understand how God is unlimited by anything, or infinite, free, self-determined, and not determined by anything other than himself contrary to his own sovereign purposes."[220] Thus, aseity addresses God's independence, self-existence, and self-sufficiency. It provides the basis for the comprehension of God's activity in the purpose of creation, as well as the affairs of mankind.

Before enlarging upon the doctrine of creation it is important to emphasize that God did not need to create the world. Norman Geisler writes, "God did not need to create-an infinite, perfect Being needs nothing. God was not lonely, for as a triunity of persons-Father, Son, and Holy Spirit- God had absolutely perfect fellowship within Himself. He did not have to seek any companionship elsewhere."[221] In addition, God is both ontologically and psychologically *a se.* James Beilby explains:

> God is ontologically *a se.* He is uncaused, without beginning, not dependent on an external person, principle, or metaphysical reality for his existence. Second, God is psychologically *a se.* There is no lack or need in God. He is fully self-satisfied, not needing anything outside of himself to be happy or fulfilled.[222]

---

[220] Elwell, *Evangelical Dictionary of Theology,* 453.

[221] Geisler, *Systematic Theology in One Volume,* 639.

[222] James Beilby, "Divine Aseity, Divine Freedom: A Conceptual Problem for Edwardsian-Calvinism," *JETS* 47 (2004): 647.

To show the conflict between God's sovereignty, as manifested through His aseity, and divine determinism, two questions need to be asked and answered. The first question to address is: Why did God create and specifically why did He create mankind? Most would readily agree with Isaiah 43:7 that man's purpose in being created was to bring glory to God. Apostle Paul reiterates that purpose in 1 Corinthians 6:20 where he emphasizes man should glorify God in body and spirit. Clearly, God is worthy to be praised and glorified, and for this end was man created.

Beilby makes an acute observation in his great article about divine aseity and the freedom of God in creation. He observes:

> If God's purpose in creation is to accomplish a task-bringing glory to himself-that he both desires and cannot accomplish without creation, it seems that God becomes dependent on creation to accomplish this task ... Thus, the tension exists between aseity and the claim that God's purposes in creating was to bring glory to himself.[223]

This point of conflict and contradiction is exposed by professor Thomas McCall. He quotes the words of John Piper, a popular Calvinist author and teacher, who expressed his belief that God has ordained all things for his own glory. Piper describes his perspective:

> We rebel against the very idea that God predestines for his own glory and thus renders it necessary that creatures made in his image will be damned so that he can look good, and our very rebellion is further proof that we want to be God. On the other hand, when we come to the place where we recognize just

---

[223] Ibid., 649.

who is and who is not sovereign, we understand that
it is right for God to pursue his own glory this way.[224]

This contradiction to the very nature of God culminates in the abhorrent teaching that God, out of necessity, in order to demonstrate his glory, predestinated sin so that he could show his wrath on the non-elect for the embellishment of his grace to the elect.

Was God free to create? Beilby gives the logical conclusion to the Calvinistic position: "If God must express his glory and his glory requires the expression of attributes expressible only in creation, then it follows that to express his glory … he must create."[225] There are some troubling implications to this perspective. For one thing, it posits that the maximization of God's grace and glory is magnified the most in the context of sin and suffering. Furthermore, it portrays God as a wicked tyrant who needs to create people in order to damn them eternally.

The grandeur of sovereignty and grace, as advocated by Reformed theology, tramples on the omni-benevolence, goodness, and justice of God. Clearly, to believe that the fulfillment of God's glory is possible *only* through his manifested attributes is to insist that God had to create and is thus dependent upon his own creation.

God's choice to create must be self-determined and free from arbitrariness and external factors. Distinguished theologian Carl Henry noted:

> Evangelical theology affirms aseity; it declares that
> the universe is not necessary either to divine being
> or to divine perfection. God stands free of such
> dependence; he alone, moreover, stands completely
> and intrinsically independent of the created order …

---

[224] Qtd in Thomas H. McCall, "I Believe in Divine Sovereignty," *Trinity Journal* 29 (2008): 214.
[225] Beilby, "Divine Aseity, Divine Freedom: A Conceptual Problem for Edwardsian-Calvinism," 654.

> Creation is not an absolute necessity for God, nor
> does the universe exhaustively reveal him.[226]

Thus, divine aseity not only requires self-determinism but also demands that there be no internal necessity for God to create. This would violate the nature of God by contradicting His self-sufficiency and self-existence and make Him depend upon that which He created. However, as Kyle Fedler maintained, "In declaring the absolute sovereignty of Yahweh, Genesis 1 also tells us that God does not create out of necessity. God was not forced to create the world, nor does God need the world in order to be God."[227]

The Sovereignty of God and Omnipotence

The omnipotence of God denotes that He has all power to do whatever is possible to do. However, omnipotence functions in harmony with the other attributes of God to prevent any contradiction in the nature of God. The absolute sovereignty of God manifests itself in accordance with God's free will and omnipotence without invalidating, violating, or subordinating any other attribute. Herein lies another problem with divine determinism, which implies the arbitrary sovereignty of God. By suggesting that God can do anything He wants to do even though those actions violate other attributes, Calvinism confuses and contorts the very understanding of the nature of God. Unger agreed, "By ascribing to God absolute power, it is not meant that God is free from all the restraints of reason and morality, as some have taught, but that He is able to do everything that is in harmony with His wise and holy and perfect nature."[228]

---

[226] Carl F. H. Henry, *God, Revelation and Authority – Volume V* (Waco, TX: Word Books, Publishers, 1982), 12.

[227] Kyle D. Fedler, *Exploring Christian Ethics* (Louisville, KY: Westminster John Knox Press, 2006), 70.

[228] Unger, *Unger's Bible Dictionary*, 808.

To advocate the interrelationship of omnipotence with God's other attributes does not in any way diminish the omnipotence of God. Biblical evidence and exhortations declaring the omnipotence of God provide great hope and comfort to the Christian. For instance, the omnipotence of God is seen in Genesis 1:1 where God creates the heaven and earth ex nihilo (out of nothing). The psalmist declares in Psalms 115:3 that, "Our God is in the heavens: he hath done whatsoever he hath pleased." Ephesians 1:19 strengthens the faith of the Christian as it reads, "And what is the exceeding greatness of his power to us-ward who believe, according to the working of his mighty power." Hebrews 1:3 reminds the believer that Christ upholds all things by the word of his power. From the Scriptures comes the revelation that God, who is omnipotent, is also involved in the affairs of His creation. God is not only the originating Cause; He is also the operating or sustaining Cause. Thus, the involvement of God in his own Creation displays a personal God, who, even though he is omnipotent, is capable of having a relationship with those he has created. The omni-benevolence, omniscience, and omni-sapience of God allows for the harmonious relationship to be sustained because God does not manifest His omnipotence arbitrarily. Evans and Manis helpfully clarify how God's omnipotence relates to his other attributes: "God's omnipotence must then be understood as the power to do whatever is logically possible and consistent with God's own essential characteristics. God's power is still infinite in the sense of being unlimited by anything outside himself."[229]

An example of divine deterministic arbitrary omnipotence is captured in a statement by John Piper. He stated, "God's love for us is ultimately a way of loving himself better. Thus, God takes the righteous course of action and seeks his own glory by creating the world where the divinely-determined ratio of rapes, earthquakes, damnation, and salvation is such that it works to glorify him maximally."[230] The problems with this egregious statement are

---

[229] C. Stephens Evans and R. Zachary Manis, *Philosophy of Religion* (Downers Grove, IL: IVP Academic, 2009), 39.

[230] Qtd in McCall, "I Believe in Divine Sovereignty," 216.

many. First, in 1 Corinthians 13:5 "love seeketh not her own." Also, in John 15:12 Jesus stated that, "ye love one another, as I have loved you." Mankind understands love as taught by the word of God, demonstrated by Jesus, and experienced through the Holy Spirit. This statement clearly contradicts the omni-benevolence of God. In addition, how can an omnibenevolent God obtain more love?

Second, God is fully satisfied and maximized in His glory from all eternity. To suggest that God needed anything in creation to maximize himself or his glory contradicts the aseity of God. Consider the wise insight from theologian Thomas Oden:

> Since Christian teaching affirms the goodness and wisdom of God in enabling and empowering human freedom, it cannot be satisfied with a determinism that denies human freedom or asserts God's almighty power or influence in such a way as to eliminate all other influences; or a view of chance that denies divine purposefulness; or a view of fate that denies divine benevolence.[231]

Third, to posit the idea that a righteous action by a holy God brought divinely determined rape and damnation into the world to glorify himself maximally is blasphemous. God is purity of Being. God is totally set apart from all evil and could not predestinate or foreordain that which he hates. Biblical truth and moral law condemn such fallacious thinking. Clearly, this statement offends and contradicts the very holy nature of God. If God determines everything, then he determines things to occur in a manner that both pleases and distresses himself. God is not the author of confusion yet the argument that divine sovereignty equals divine determinism creates confusion and contradictions. For instance, God hates sin yet predetermined it for His glorification. A good illustration of the absurdity that Calvinism creates is expressed by Piper, who

---

[231] Thomas C. Oden, *The Living God-Systematic Theology-Volume One* (San Francisco, CA: HarperCollins Publishers, 1987), 278.

argued "that God's emotional life is complex beyond our ability to comprehend ... therefore we should not stumble over the fact that God does and does not take pleasure in the death of the wicked."[232]

Concluding Comments on the Sovereignty of God

Three objectives were established in this chapter to properly explain the sovereignty of God. The first objective was to fulfill the purpose of defining the sovereignty of God doctrinally, biblically, and theologically. The second objective was to refute divine determinism and expose the Calvinistic error of making it synonymous with divine sovereignty. The third objective was to clearly show that libertarian free will harmonizes the sovereignty of God and human responsibility. To achieve these objectives, arbitrary sovereignty, moral law, aseity, and omnipotence were used to justify the clear definition and understanding of absolute sovereignty. A few concluding comments must be made in relation to the sovereignty of God.

Robert Shank noted, "One of the great fallacies of Calvinism is the assumption that unconditional particular election is an essential corollary-virtually the sine qua non-of the sovereignty of God."[233] Earl Martin offers insight into a logical fallacy of Calvinism: "I must think of his omniscience in such a way that his knowledge does not cause me to confuse certainty and foreknowledge with necessity and predestination. Knowledge is not causation, and foreknowledge is not predeterminism."[234] Finally, God is a gracious, covenant-making God who manifests and exercises His sovereignty through His attributes. God cannot violate His nature or exercise arbitrary sovereignty. For example, Robert Picirilli remarked:

> The unconditionality of God's sovereign 'decisions' (plan, purpose) does not necessarily mean that

[232] Qtd in McCall, "I Believe in Divine Sovereignty," 210-211.
[233] Shank, *Elect in the Son*, 143.
[234] Martin, *Toward Understanding God*, 60.

all the ends God has purposed are achieved unconditionally or necessarily. What seems clear is that God has unconditionally (sovereignly) decreed to administer salvation conditionally. And 'conditionally' includes true contingency ... We may say, then, that God unconditionally decreed that salvation be conditional."[235]

Therefore, man has libertarian free will to choose or reject God's plan of salvation. God created self-determination, and God is no less sovereign because man has free will.

---

[235] Picirilli, *Grace, Faith, Free Will*, 45.

CHAPTER 6

Is Free Will for Real?

Topics of free will and predestination are often quite heated. People have strong opinions about where they stand on this theological debate. Erwin Lutzer tells a humorous story that relays this reality:

> Perhaps you heard about the group of theologians who were discussing the doctrines of predestination and free will. When the argument became heated, the dissidents split into two groups. One man, unable to make up his mind which group to join, slipped into the predestination crowd. Challenged as to why he was there, he replied, "I came of my own free will." The group retorted, "Free will! You don't belong here!" So he retreated to the opposing group and when asked why he switched responded, "I was sent here." "Get out," they stormed. "You can't join us unless you come of your own free will!" The confused man was left out in the cold.[236]

---

[236] Erwin Lutzer, *The Doctrines That Divide* (Grand Rapids, MI: Kregel Publications, 1998), 153.

It seems that this debate has not diminished in recent years. Unfortunately, this hypothetical story represents what many people think about this issue: To believe in free will is to not believe in predestination, or to believe in predestination is to not believe in free will. This, of course, would be true, if predestination were defined as the unchangeable ordination of "whatsoever comes to pass."[237] However, predestination is not used in the Scriptures in this way. According to William Klein, "God has predestined certain outcomes for the elect, those who are his people; however, predestination does not specify the identities of those who will become his people."[238] It does not refer to "God's choice of who will become his children; instead, predestination concerns what goals or outcomes God has determined beforehand for his people."[239] In other words, predestination deals with *what* will happen to those who are in Christ (Ephesians 1:5,11; Romans 8:29), but it does not address *who* will be in Christ.

Christians must gladly affirm both predestination and free will, for these are significant biblical doctrines. It saddens me when certain Christian leaders are either ignorant or uninterested in what the Bible teaches about this particular issue. For instance, one preacher informed me, "Brother, we don't believe in predestination!" He stated this without emphasizing that he rejects the Calvinistic notion of predestination. For any Christian, especially a person interested in rightly dividing the Scriptures, to assert that he doesn't believe in a very biblical word (predestination) is troubling beyond comprehension. Even though he is wrong in his understanding of predestination, R. C. Sproul said it well:

> If we are to be biblical, then, the issue is not whether we should have a doctrine of predestination or not, but what kind we should embrace. If the Bible is the Word of God, nor mere human speculation, and if God himself declares that there is such a thing as

---

[237] Westminster Confession of Faith.

[238] Klein, *The New Chosen People*, 270.

[239] Ibid., 163.

predestination, then it follows irresistibly that we must embrace some doctrine of predestination.[240]

So, don't let the terms predestination, election, or sovereignty scare you! These biblical concepts are consistent with free will and should not be denied or deemphasized. Rightly understood, they highlight the majesty and wisdom of our great Creator whose ways are past finding out. In this chapter, we will investigate what free will is and why every Christian should believe in it.

What is free will?

It is not exactly correct to say that Calvinists don't believe in free will. Without a doubt, Calvinism does teach that everything is determined by God. A classic statement of this position is found in chapter III of the Westminster Confession of Faith, "God, from all eternity, did, by the most wise and holy counsel of his own will, freely, and unchangeably ordain *whatsoever comes to pass.*" Various Calvinist theologians, both past and present, support this position with pride. Paul Helm, in his book *The Providence of God*, writes, "Not only is every atom and molecule, every thought and desire kept in being by God, but every twist and turn of each of these is under the direct control of God."[241] R. C. Sproul believes that "if there is one single molecule in this universe running around loose, totally free of God's sovereignty, then we have no guarantee that a single promise of God will ever be fulfilled."[242]

Thus, Calvinistic theology insists that everything- literally everything- was determined by God before the foundations of the world, and no event in history could be different than it actually is. This might seem like a ridiculous caricature of a well-known and supported theological position, but it is indeed an accurate

---

[240] Sproul, *Chosen by God*, 11.

[241] Qtd in Lennox, *Determined to Believe?*, 54.

[242] Sproul, *Chosen by God*, 27.

representation of what Calvinists mean by divine sovereignty. Consistent Calvinism asserts that the fact you are reading this sentence at this precise moment in history is just as determined as the crucifixion of Jesus Christ. It's no wonder why some Christian philosophers identify Calvinism as "divine determinism."[243]

You might wonder, then, how it is incorrect to state that Calvinists don't believe in free will, given their view of God's sovereignty. The reason is that, *while they do not deny free will, per se, they do redefine free will.* This view is known as "compatibilism" and is an attempt to reconcile free will and determinism. R. C. Sproul advocates this position in his influential book *Chosen by God.* To get around the obvious dilemma of all-encompassing determinism, he reinterprets free will to be the "ability to choose what we want."[244] According to Sproul, and other compatibilists, a person will always choose according to his strongest inclination at the moment of decision. Sproul concludes, "Our choices are determined by our desires."[245] In other words, we choose as we do because that is what we most want to choose.

Let's look at an example to help you understand how a Calvinist views free will. Suppose you visit a local ice cream shop on a warm summer afternoon. At this specific ice cream shop, there are twelve flavors. However, you only like three flavors that they have available: chocolate, strawberry, and vanilla. You have chosen each of these flavors before, so the decision is extremely difficult to make. Finally, after a few minutes of careful thinking, you choose chocolate ice cream. Why did you choose chocolate ice cream? To a Calvinist, you chose chocolate ice cream because you wanted chocolate ice cream more than you wanted strawberry or vanilla ice cream. In a nutshell, this is what free will means according to the Calvinist.

Is this free will, though? A moment's inspection of this definition should lead to a question: What determines our desires? If we are free to choose according to our desires, but our desires are determined by forces outside of our control (i.e., God), then aren't our actions

---

[243] Olson, *Against Calvinism*, 70-101.
[244] Sproul, *Chosen by God.*, 54.
[245] Ibid.

still determined? Braxton Hunter is spot on in his description of compatibilism: "Man is free to do whatever he wants, but not free to want whatever he wants. That is to say, man has freedom to exercise his will in accordance with his desires, but he has no control over those desires."[246] For Calvinists to state that humans have the freedom to choose according to the strongest inclinations without acknowledging that those inclinations are determined by God is dishonest and a classic case of what Jerry Walls calls "misleading rhetoric."[247] The Calvinist tries to camouflage his belief in determinism by inventing a version of free will that makes his position more palatable.

The commonsensical view of free will, on the other hand, is libertarian freedom.[248] John Wesley referred to this view of freedom as the "liberty of contradiction" and defined it as "the power of choosing either to do or not to do" something.[249] Roger Olson gives a good definition of libertarian freedom: "When an agent (a human or God) acts freely in the libertarian sense, nothing outside the self (including physical realities within the body) is causing it."[250] Most people would probably find this to agree with their sense of reality. You have the freedom to marry Jane or Amanda, to drive a truck or a van, to live in the suburbs or the city, and to read a book or go for a walk. You are the one who determines which choice you make, and after you make a choice, upon reflection, you believe that you could have chosen differently than you actually chose.

Let's return to our ice cream example with this view of free will in mind. You are at the same ice cream shop, and you still only like

---

[246] David L. Allen, Eric Hankins, and Adam Harwood, *Anyone Can Be Saved* (Eugene, OR: Wipf & Stock), 120.

[247] Jerry Walls, "Why No Classical Theist, Let Alone Orthodox Christian, Should Ever Be a Compatibilist," *Philosophia Christi* 13 (2011): 101.

[248] Walls and Dongell, *Why I Am Not a Calvinist*, 103.

[249] John Wesley, *The Works of John Wesley- Vol. X* (Grand Rapids, MI: Baker Book House, 1978), 463.

[250] Roger Olson, *Arminian Theology: Myths and Realities* (Downers Grove, IL: IVP Academic, 2006), 75.

chocolate, vanilla, and strawberry. Today, you chose strawberry ice cream instead of the other flavors. Why, according to libertarian free will, did you choose strawberry ice cream? The answer is astonishingly simple. You chose strawberry ice cream because that's the one you chose. Libertarian freedom does not deny the existence of internal or external factors, but it readily affirms that the choice rests in your hands. You are not enslaved by your desires. You certainly do have desires, and those desires do influence your choice, but your choice is determined by you, not simply by your desires. Given the same set of circumstances, you could have also chosen chocolate or vanilla ice cream.

For the rest of this chapter, five arguments will be presented in defense of libertarian free will. These five arguments are the following:

1. It makes sense of the Bible.
2. It accords with our experience.
3. It allows for moral responsibility.
4. It preserves God's integrity.
5. It was the predominant view of the early church.

Before articulating these five arguments, it does seem ironic that those who deny this view of free will, including Calvinists, use this view of free will in recruiting other people. John Lennox states this perfectly, "It is common for determinists to try to convince non-determinists to convert to determinism. But that assumes that the non-determinists are free to convert, and therefore their non-determinism is not determined in the first place."[251] This, of course,

---

[251] Lennox, *Determined to Believe?*, 60. This argument is similar to a paragraph in Norman Geisler, *Chosen but Free* (Minneapolis, MN: Bethany House Publishers, 2010), 43-44: "The fact is freedom is undeniable, for if everything were determined, then so would determinists be determined to believe that we are not free. But determinists believe that determinism is true and non-determinism is false. Further, they believe that all non-determinists ought to change their view and become determinists. This

doesn't necessarily entail that libertarian free will is true, but it does highlight the strength of the position. In a sense, Calvinists affirm libertarian free will by denying it. When a Calvinist tries to persuade other Christians that Calvinism is true, he is assuming that these Christians have the freedom to accept Calvinism, which is a view of freedom that his theological system denies.

It makes sense of the Bible

Any doctrine a Christian believes should be derived from the Scriptures. The church upholds the sole authority of the Bible by studying the word of God in order to know what it teaches for the purpose of making this teaching known. We minimize the importance of the Scriptures and undermine its sufficiency by believing and teaching ideas that are unbiblical at best and anti-biblical at worst. With that said, libertarian free will seems to be assumed everywhere in the pages of Scripture. If genuine free will is false, then the Scriptures are hopelessly convoluted, and God, who is the author of this book, is portrayed as an incompetent imbecile who has miserably failed by writing terribly incoherent sentences that render it impossible to know what he actually wants.

Here are a few passages of Scripture that require libertarian free will in order to make meaningful sense:

> Yea, they have chosen their own ways, and their soul delighteth in their abominations. I also will choose their delusions, and will bring their fears upon them; because when I called, none did answer; when I spake, they did not hear: but they did evil before mine eyes, and chose that in which I delighted not (Isaiah 66:3,4).

---

implies that non-determinists are free to change their view- which is contrary to determinism. Thus it follows that determinism is false, since it is contradictory to its own claim."

O Jerusalem, Jerusalem, thou that killest the prophets, and stonest them which are sent unto thee, how often would I have gathered thy children together, even as a hen gathereth her chickens under her wings, and ye would not! (Matthew 23:37).

I call heaven and earth to record this day against you, that I have set before you life and death, blessing and cursing: therefore choose life, that both thou and thy seed may live (Deuteronomy 30:19).

If it seem evil unto you to serve the Lord, choose you this day whom ye will serve; whether the gods which your fathers served that were on the other side of the flood, or the gods of the Amorites, in whose land ye dwell: but as for me and my house, we will serve the Lord (Joshua 24:15).

And God said unto him in a dream, Yea, I know that thou didst this in the integrity of thy heart; for I also withheld thee from sinning against me: therefore suffered I thee not to touch her. Now therefore restore the man his wife; for he is a prophet, and he shall pray for thee, and thou shalt live: and if thou restore her not, know thou that thou shalt surely die, thou, and all that are thine (Genesis 20:6,7).

Notwithstanding I have a few things against thee, because thou sufferest that woman Jezebel, which calleth herself a prophetess, to teach and to seduce my servants to commit fornication, and to eat things sacrificed unto idols. And I gave her space to repent of her fornication; and she repented not. (Revelation 2:20,21).

The Lord God commanded the man, saying, Of every tree of the garden thou mayest freely eat: but of the tree of the knowledge of good and evil, thou shalt not eat of it: for in the day that thou eatest thereof thou shalt surely die (Genesis 2:16,17).

Come now, and let us reason together, saith the Lord: though your sins be as scarlet, they shall be as white as snow; though they be red like crimson, they shall be as wool. If ye be willing and obedient, ye shall eat the good of the land: but if ye refuse and rebel, ye shall be devoured with the sword: for the mouth of the Lord hath spoken it (Isaiah 1:18-20).

And it shall come to pass, if they will diligently learn the ways of my people, to swear by my name, The LORD liveth; as they taught my people to swear by Baal; then shall they be built in the midst of my people. But if they will not obey, I will utterly pluck up and destroy that nation, saith the LORD (Jeremiah 12:16,17).

I submit that the only way that these verses have sensible meanings is if libertarian free will is a reality. If, for example, Jerusalem (Matthew 23:37) could literally not do otherwise than she actually did, Jesus' weeping becomes a charade. As Steve Lemke observes, "His apparent lament over Jerusalem would have been just a disingenuous act, a cynical show because he knew that God had not and would not give these lost persons the necessary conditions for their salvation."[252] It seems that even the little word *if* serves as a powerful refutation of the Calvinistic view of free will.

There is, though, one passage that directly contradicts the compatibilist version of freedom. Again, free will, according to many Calvinists, is the ability to do what you want to do. Apparently, you

---

[252] Allen and Lemke, *Whosoever Will*, 120.

always choose according to your strongest desire. However, is this always true? Not in the mind of Paul. In Romans 7, he laments, "For that which I do I allow not: for what I would, that do I not; but what I hate, that do I … For the good that I would I do not: but the evil which I would not, that I do" (Romans 7:15,19). Here, Paul openly admits that, sometimes, there are some things he does that he doesn't want to do and that there are some things he doesn't do that he wants to do. But, if compatibilism is true, don't we always choose according to our greatest desires?

As a matter of fact, Sproul addresses this passage in *Chosen by God*. He confesses that "it sounds as if, under the inspiration of God the Holy Spirit, Paul is teaching clearly that there are times in which he acts against his strongest inclination."[253] How does Sproul respond to this evident quandary? He continues, "It is extremely unlikely that the apostle is here giving us a revelation about the technical operation of the will."[254] That's undoubtedly correct, probably because nowhere in Paul's writings does he offer a detailed discussion of the "technical operation of the will", but Sproul's response does not solve the Calvinist's dilemma. Yes, Paul does not elaborate in Romans 7 on why he chooses evil, not good, even though his desire is to choose good. However, the point to emphasize is that Paul, under the inspiration of the Holy Spirit, writes a few statements that contradict the compatibilist notion of free will. It is simply false that we always choose according to our greatest desire.

It accords with our experience

Another argument in favor of libertarian free will is that it seems to agree with our own experiences. For instance, I *feel* as if I have genuine freedom. My consciousness tells me that I can freely make decisions. Yesterday, I went to the bank to get a new debit card because my debit card had been malfunctioning. Now, libertarian

---

[253] Sproul, *Chosen by God*, 58.
[254] Ibid.

free will states that I could have chosen to do something else, and this corresponds to what I think I could have done. I feel as if I could have waited to go to the bank today, tomorrow, or next week. Maybe my intuition is incorrect, and my visiting the bank was determined by God before the foundations of the world. However, it appears to me that my action to go to the bank was not determined, but within my power to choose otherwise than what I did choose.

I would reckon that this intuition is universal. Everyone thinks that he has free will. Granted, this does not imply that everybody has the same number of options. Living in America greatly increases the types of decisions we must make. A quick visit to the local grocery store will verify the validity of this statement. Nevertheless, even citizens of third-world countries must make choices every day, and my contention is that everyone considers himself to be free to choose, regardless of the decision. Again, this intuition could be false, but that doesn't negate the universality of our sense of freedom.

Steve Lemke argues that libertarian free will "squares with our experience of decision making in real life. As we make decisions, we believe that we are genuinely making a decision between real alternatives, not just doing what we most desire," as compatibilists argue.[255] Lemke offers an analogy of what our decision making looks like:

> Most of us picture our decision making as being like a president and his cabinet of advisors. The advisors may argue with each other about what choice should be made, just as our emotions, desires, and rational judgment may cry out for us to act in a particular way. In the end, however, it is the president who decides what will be done. Likewise, in our own lives, though our desires are a powerful force, it is the self or person who decides what we will do, not just our desires.[256]

---

[255] Allen, Hankins, and Harwood, *Anyone Can Be Saved*, 175.
[256] Ibid.

But, what if this intuition is wrong? What if we aren't free like we think we are? What if our actions are determined, and our sense of freedom is illusory? There are *two* fundamental issues if this universal notion of freedom is false.

The first issue would be whether we could trust anything else about our experiences. John Miley brings this problem to the forefront in arguing for free will.[257] He writes, "If there be not the reality of freedom this common consciousness is deceptive. *If it may be so in this case, so may it be in others.* Consciousness would thus be discredited, and no ground of assured knowledge could remain."[258] Some Calvinists might find this argument ludicrous and unconvincing, but to my mind, it appears to be a necessary implication of Calvinistic theology. If our consciousness has deceived us into thinking that we are free when, in reality, our actions are not free, what else in our consciousness could be considered reliable and trustworthy? Our experience of pain? Of love? Of joy? Perhaps, even our sense of existence is not real but illusory. It is problematic to deny that our sense of freedom is genuine.

A second complication with rejecting a libertarian view of free will is that it makes God ultimately responsible for this misconception about ourselves. Now, if evolution were true, and we are the byproduct of millions of years of random processes, it wouldn't be too difficult to accept that our sense of reality would be a little skewed. However, for those who affirm the existence of God, it becomes troublesome as to why God would give everyone (not just you and me) a mistaken understanding of themselves. In a powerful article exposing the biblical and philosophical plight of compatibilism, Jerry Walls lays out the dilemma, "A theist who holds that God is perfectly good and that he is the ultimate designer of human nature should be much more reluctant to think that God has implanted within the tendency to believe deeply misleading things."[259] He concludes, "If

---

[257] Miley, *Systematic Theology- Vol. 2*, 283. Italics mine.

[258] Ibid. Italics mine.

[259] Walls, "Why No Classical Theist, Let Alone Orthodox Christian, Should Ever Be a Compatibilist," 79.

our clearest, most vivid perception and intuitions are fundamentally misleading where they bear on morally significant matters such as freedom and personal responsibility, this is hard to square with God's perfect goodness."[260] Affirming that the universal intuition of free will is false and misleading would seem to suggest that God has led everyone to believe a lie about themselves, but such a suggestion would directly contradict the biblical claim that God does not (and cannot) lie (Titus 1:2; Hebrews 6:18).

We feel like we have true freedom. Now, it is important to emphasize that this argument doesn't have to be true in order for it to be effective. We perceive that we have the freedom to act differently than we actually have acted in the past or will act in the future. I think that I could have chosen to stay at home instead of going to the bank. If this intuition is universal, and Calvinism is also true, then why did God give us a false sense of ourselves? Fortunately, this sense of freedom not only agrees with our personal experiences but also possesses strong biblical support, provides an explanation for moral responsibility, and protects the holy goodness of God.

It allows for moral responsibility

There is a close connection between freedom and responsibility. This is seen in the fact that only if someone could have chosen otherwise can he be considered responsible for his actions. Even the judicial laws of our country are founded upon this basic understanding. As Walls and Dongell note, "A person cannot be held morally responsible for an act unless he or she was free to perform that act and free to refrain from it."[261]

From a Calvinistic perspective, every sin committed is done *freely* because the person committing the sin wants to sin. The murderer murders because he desires to murder, the adulterer cheats on his wife because he wants to cheat on his wife, and the homosexual is a

---

[260] Ibid.
[261] Walls and Dongell, *Why I Am Not a Calvinist*, 105.

homosexual because he wants to be a homosexual.[262] However, even though these people defy God's will *freely*, the sinful desires that lead to sinful behavior have been determined by God, and it was literally impossible for them to have acted differently. In a deterministic system, there are no contingencies. Everything is done in accordance with God's secret decree, so even though all sins committed today, tomorrow, and yesterday could not have been resisted, God still holds people responsible because they were doing what they wanted to do.

Most people will find this to be objectionable. And I agree. It runs against our very sense of justice. In relation to this basic intuition, Jerry Walls presents what he calls "the provenance principle":

> When the actions of a person are entirely determined by another intelligent being who intentionally determines (manipulates) the person to act exactly as the other being wishes, then the person cannot rightly be held accountable and punished for his actions.[263]

Could anyone disagree with this? Would a Calvinist object? Would he argue that this applies to every other situation in the universe besides the all-encompassing decree of God? Is God held to a different standard of morality than his creatures? John Calvin seemed to think so. He wrote, "It is perverse to measure divine by the standard of human justice."[264] But doesn't this directly contradict the teaching of the Bible that insists that we should be like God?[265] Our sense of justice is derived from our being fashioned in the image of God (Genesis 9:6; James 3:9). If we are commanded to be like

---

[262] I once asked a Calvinist what he would say to a homosexual who stated "God made me this way." Given his theological framework, can this really be denied?

[263] Walls, "Why No Classical Theist, Let Alone Orthodox Christian, Should Ever Be a Compatibilist," 87.

[264] Calvin, *Institutes of the Christian Religion*, 651.

[265] Matthew 5:48; Leviticus 11:45; Luke 6:36.

God, but it is morally acceptable for God to determine that certain individuals will commit gross iniquities, why is it morally *unacceptable* for human beings to determine other people to commit the very same atrocities? On the contrary, just as it is morally reprehensible for a person to manipulate someone to commit evil, so it would also be morally reprehensible for God to determine his creatures to commit evil.

Another line of evidence that moral responsibility requires human freedom is that the Bible instructs us that the good and evil actions of mankind will be rewarded and punished, respectively. But does the Bible inform us of a similar judgment for the animals or the plants? Of course not! Why, though? If, according to Calvinism, our actions are just as determined as those of the animals, yet we will be held accountable for those actions, why won't the animals also be judged? As John Wesley observed:

> God is a rewarder of them that diligently seek him. But he cannot reward the sun for shining, because the sun is not a free agent. Neither could he reward us, for letting our light shine before men, if we acted as necessarily as the sun. All reward, as well as all punishment, pre-supposes free-agency; and whatever creature is incapable of choice, is incapable of either one or the other.[266]

The very idea of rewards and punishments points to the existence of free moral agency. It is acceptable, then, for Geisler to ask: "Why eulogize Mother Teresa and vilify Hitler if they could not help doing what they did? Why blame Pol Pot and praise Martin Luther King if they had no free choice in the matter?"[267] The Calvinists respond that the reason why this is possible is because they were doing what they wanted to do. This loses its force once it is acknowledged that those very desires were also determined by God and that it was

---

[266] Wesley, *The Works of John Wesley- Vol. X*, 362.

[267] Geisler, *Chosen But Free*, 43.

literally impossible for Adolf Hitler to have *not* been a murderous despot.

It preserves God's integrity

This leads to the next reason to affirm libertarian free will. If everything has been determined by God, then it is difficult to see how he is not also the author and originator of sin. Roger Olson presents the Calvinistic dilemma in his book *Against Calvinism*. He writes, "All Calvinists say that God is not responsible for sin and evil even though he foreordains and renders them certain, and that creatures are responsible even though they could not do otherwise than they do."[268] To simultaneously affirm that God has determined everything *and* that he is not responsible for sin only makes sense to a Calvinist. To everyone else, if God determined everything, including sin and evil, then he is responsible for this sin and evil, and his integrity is irreparably damaged.

This can be illustrated by looking at the Fall.[269] A non-Calvinistic interpretation of Adam and Eve's first sin is that God created mankind with the capacity to make genuine choices. Unlike the rest of creation, he fashioned men and women after his likeness. A significant component of being created in God's image is the ability to freely choose. Along with this freedom, again, comes tremendous responsibility. God presented Adam and Eve with a moral requirement carrying severe consequences as a result of disobedience. God did not want them to sin, neither did he manipulate them into sinning. He allowed them the freedom to choose to obey or disobey. Unfortunately, they chose to rebel against God's command. Nevertheless, God's reputation is preserved because Adam and Eve freely sinned in spite of God's warning and provision. It was their choice, and they were held responsible for their sinful behavior.

---

[268] Olson, *Against Calvinism*, 94.

[269] "The Fall" is used in reference to the entrance of sin into the world. It points to Adam and Eve's first sin.

How does a Calvinist answer the Fall? Some, recognizing that this is obviously an excruciating problem for theistic determinism, appeal to mystery. This is the approach of R. C. Sproul. When he addresses why Adam and Eve, who were undoubtedly created good, chose to sin, he responds, "I don't know. Nor have I found anyone yet who does know."[270] This pious appeal to ignorance is necessary for Calvinists who seek to affirm God's goodness and moral integrity while also insisting that he has determined all that comes to pass.

This problem gets worse. Again, Calvinists typically are compatibilists and define free will as the ability to choose according to our desires. If this is true, then where did Adam's first desire to sin originate? Since Adam and Eve were created as good creatures, the desire to sin could not have come from them. Wouldn't Calvinists have to say that God put the first desire to sin in Adam? At the very least, Calvinists must insist that Adam's sinful behavior was determined by God, and he literally could not have resisted the temptation. With this in mind, how is God *not* the author of sin, and how can Adam, or anyone else, be held responsible for their sins if they had to sin? These types of questions lead many Calvinists, including a prominent Calvinist like R. C. Sproul, to appeal to mystery when, in reality, it is contradictory to claim that God is good even though he determined sin to enter into his creation.

Gunther Juncker has written a devastating critique of Calvinism entitled "The Dilemma of Theistic Determinism." In this short article, he argues that the logical implications of theological determinism (or Calvinism), if true, mean that "God is evil and the author of evil *or* all talk of good and evil, of praise and blame, of moral responsibility,

---

[270] Sproul, in *Chosen by God*, wrote: "Before a person can commit an act of sin he must first have a desire to perform that act. The Bible tells us that evil actions flow from evil desires. But the presence of an evil desire is already sin. We sin because we are sinners. We were born with a sin nature. We are fallen creatures. But Adam and Eve were not created fallen. They had no sin nature. They were good creatures with a free will. Yet they chose to sin. Why? I don't know. Nor have I found anyone yet who does know" (pp. 30-31).

and of justice is meaningless and incomprehensible with reference to God."[271] He contends that "in a fully determined world, there can only be one sinner"- God.[272] His argument is simple and seems to be a "self-evident moral truth" that, if denied, would destroy the very foundation for morality:

1. A being who causes/determines evil is evil.
2. The God of theistic determinism is a being who causes/determines evil.
3. Therefore, the God of theistic determinism is evil.[273]

This might be why John Wesley contended that Calvinism makes God "worse that the devil, as both more false, more cruel and more unjust."[274] The portrait of God that Calvinism presents is "at best morally ambiguous and at worst a moral monster hardly distinguishable from the devil."[275] Unless humans have genuine free will, God's reputation as a good God is maligned. A fitting illustration given by Tom McCall is an accurate representation of the type of God portrayed by Calvinistic theology:

> Imagine a parent who is able to control each and every action of his children, and furthermore is able to do so by controlling their thoughts and inclinations. He is thus able to determine each and all actions taken by those children. He is also able to guarantee that they desire to do everything that they do, and this is exactly what he does. He puts them in a special playroom that contains not only toys but also gasoline and matches, and then

---

[271] Gunther H. Juncker, "The Dilemma of Theistic Determinism," *Journal for Baptist Theology & Ministry* 12 (2015): 15. Italics mine.

[272] Ibid.,18.

[273] Ibid.,17.

[274] Qtd in Olson, *Against Calvinism*, 128.

[275] Ibid., 84.

he gives them explicit instructions (with severe warnings) to avoid touching the gasoline and matches. Stepping out of sight, he determines that the children indeed begin to play with the gasoline and matches. When the playroom is ablaze and the situation desperate, he rushes in to save them (well, some of them). He breaks through the wall, grabs three of his seven children, and carries them to safety. When the rescued children calm down, they ask about their four siblings. They want to know about the others who are trapped inside, awaiting their inevitable fate. More importantly, they want to know if he can do something to rescue them as well. When they ask about the situation, their father tells them that this tragic occurrence had been determined by him, and indeed that it was a smashing success- it had worked out in exact accordance with his plan. He then reminds them of his instructions and warnings, and he reminds them further that they willingly violated his commands. They should be grateful for their rescue, and they should understand that the others got what they deserved. When they begin to sob, he weeps with them; he tells them that he too has compassion on the doomed children (indeed, the compassion of the children for their siblings only dimly reflects his own). The children are puzzled by this, and one wants to know why such a compassionate father does not rescue the others (when it is clearly within his power to do so). His answer is this: that has happened so that everyone could see how smart he is (for being able to know how to do all this), how powerful he is (for being able to control everything and then effectively rescue them), how merciful he is (for rescuing the children who broke the rules), and how just he is (for leaving the others to their fate in the burning playroom). And, he says, "This is the righteous thing for me to do, because it allows me took as good as I should look."[276]

It was the predominant view of the early church

It would be both foolish and dangerous to believe a doctrine that nobody in the history of the church has accepted. For over two thousand years, the church has diligently studied the Scriptures. While there have been major differences amongst the different traditions in the church, there has also been tremendous similarity in doctrine. For the most part, the church has affirmed the deity of Christ, the authority of the Scriptures, the second coming of Jesus Christ, and the triune nature of God. Reading the history of church doctrine, then, serves as a safety net to guide us in our study of the Bible.

In relation to free will, the early church fathers unanimously affirmed free will. Richard Swinburne, for example, writes, "My assessment of the Christian theological tradition is that all Christian theologians of the first four centuries believe in human free will in the libertarian sense."[277] The first person to disagree with this unanimity was Augustine in the fifth century, and his disagreement did not arise until later in his life. In his early writings, even he wrote in support of genuine free will. The following quotations are pulled from the various writings of these church fathers to demonstrate that there was broad confirmation of libertarian free will in the early church.[278]

---

[276] Tom McCall, "We Believe in God's Sovereign Goodness," *Trinity Journal* 29 (2008): 241-242.

[277] Qtd in Allen, Hankins, and Harwood, *Anyone Can Be Saved*, 39.

[278] These quotations are taken from Geisler, *Chosen But Free*, 189-198.

Justin Martyr (AD 100-165)

God, wishing men and angels to follow his will, resolved to create them free to do righteousness. But if the Word of God foretells that some angels and men shall certainly be punished, it did so because it foreknew that they would be unchangeably (wicked), but not because God created them so. So if they repent, all who wish for it can obtain mercy from God.

Irenaeus (AD 130-200)

If then it were not in our power to do or not to do these things, what reason had the apostle, and much more the Lord Himself, to give us counsel to do some things and to abstain from others? But because man is possessed of free will from the beginning, and God is possessed of free will in whose likeness man was created, advice is always given to him to keep fast the good, which thing is done by means of obedience to God.

Bardaisan of Syria (c. AD 154-222)

How is it that God did not so make us that we should not sin and incur condemnation? If man had been made so, he would not have belonged to himself but would have been the instrument of him that moved him ... And how, in that case, would a man differ from a harp, on which another plays; or from a ship, which another guides: where the praise and the blame reside in the hand of the performer or the steersman ... They being only instruments made for the use of him in whom is the skill? But God, in his benignity, chose not so to make man; but by freedom He exalted him above many of His creatures.

Tertullian (AD 155-225)

I find, then, that man was by God constituted free, master of his own will and power; indicating the presence of God's image and likeness in him by nothing so well as by this constitution of his nature ... You will find that when He sets before man good and evil, life and death, that the entire course of discipline is arranged in precepts by God's calling men from sin, and threatening and exhorting them; and this on no other ground than that man is free, with a will either for obedience or resistance ...

Novatian of Rome (c. AD 200-258)

He also placed man at the head of the world, and man, too, made in the image of God, to whom he imparted mind, and reason, and foresight, that he might imitate God; and although the first elements of his body were earthly yet the substance was inspired by a heavenly and divine breathing. And when He had given him all things for His service, He willed that he alone should be free. And lest, again, an unbounded freedom should fall into peril, He laid down a command, in which man was taught that there was no evil in the fruit of the tree; but he was forewarned that evil would arise if perchance he should exercise his free will in the contempt of the law that was given.

Methodius (c. AD 260-311)

Those who decide that man is not possessed of free will, and affirm that he is governed by the unavoidable necessities of fate … are guilty of impiety toward God Himself, making Him out to be the cause and author of human evils.

Cyril of Jerusalem (c. AD 312-386)

The soul is self-governed: and though the Devil can suggest, he has not the power to compel against the will. He pictures to thee the thought of fornication: if thou wilt, thou rejectest. For if thou wert a fornicator of necessity, then for what cause did God prepare hell? If thou wert a doer of righteousness by nature and not by will, wherefore did God prepare crowns of ineffable glory?

CHAPTER 7

Does Regeneration
Precede Faith?

For any theological system, some doctrines are more foundational than others. While a few doctrines could be discarded without toppling the entire structure, other doctrines are necessary to the very existence of the system. One example of this is the doctrine of God. The Bible clearly reveals certain attributes about God, such as his love, his holiness, and his goodness. The Scriptures are unambiguous in affirming that he is great and greatly to be praised (Psalm 48:1). Importantly, by declaring *who* God is, the Scriptures attest *that* God is. The biblical authors never attempt to prove God's existence. On the contrary, Moses, for instance, wrote, "In the beginning God created ..." (Genesis 1:1). According to the Scriptures, then, his existence is an unimpeachable truth.

Now, what's more foundational: that God exists, or who God is? Both of these questions, no doubt, are worthy of careful investigation and thoughtful response. However, in order to answer the second question, the first question must be true, for if God did not exist, it would be impossible to describe his character. Unless God exists, theology becomes a waste of time, money, and energy. Studying about God demands that there actually be a God to study. Thus,

God's existence is more foundational than God's attributes, because if God did not exist, then it would be preposterous to invest oneself in a lifelong examination of his nature. Fortunately, because God exists, studying about his attributes and actions is not an exercise in futility but a noble pursuit that edifies the souls of all who endeavor to better understand "the only wise God our Saviour" (Jude 25).

The same principle applies to Calvinism. TULIP isn't just five random doctrines thrown together without any consideration to their order in the acrostic. Total depravity, unconditional election, limited atonement, irresistible grace, and the perseverance of the saints follow logically, one right after the other. Therefore, if the first point of Calvinism can be proven to be erroneous, then the entire system will crumble to the ground.

That these five doctrines are intricately weaved together is not just an isolated opinion from those who oppose Calvinistic soteriology.[279] Even leading Calvinists recognize the harmony required for these doctrines to make sense. For example, in their book *The Five Points of Calvinism*, David Steele and Curtis Thomas encourage readers to "consider carefully the collective value of the evidence when *these five doctrines are viewed together as a system*":

> These doctrines are so inseparably connected that no one of them can be fully appreciated unless it is properly related to, and viewed in light of the other four; for they mutually explain and support one another. To judge these doctrines individually without relating each to the others would be like attempting to evaluate one of Rembrandt's paintings by looking at only one color at a time and never viewing the work as a whole. Do not, therefore, merely judge the Biblical evidence for each point separately, but rather consider carefully the collective value of the evidence

---

[279] Soteriology is three-dollar word that simply means "the doctrine of salvation." So, Calvinistic soteriology is the Calvinists' doctrine about salvation.

when these five doctrines are viewed together as a system. When thus properly correlated, they form a fivefold cord of unbreakable strength.[280]

One doctrine in particular that is especially essential for Calvinism to be true is the belief that regeneration comes before faith. In this chapter, we will explain why Calvinists maintain this position and examine the passages that Calvinists have used to develop this idea of pre-faith regeneration. Before doing this, though, let's look at the writings of a few prominent Calvinists to ensure that we are not misunderstanding their perspective.

A. W. Pink put it this way:

Faith is not the cause of the new birth, but the consequence of it.[281]

R. C. Sproul explains:

A cardinal point of Reformed theology is the maxim: "Regeneration precedes faith." Out nature is so corrupt, the power of sin is so great, that unless God does a supernatural work in our souls we will never choose Christ. We do not believe in order to be born again; we are born again in order that we may believe.[282]

Loraine Boettner wrote:

A man is not saved because he believes in Christ; he believes in Christ because he is saved.[283]

---

[280] Steele and Thomas, *The Five Points of Calvinism*, 24.

[281] Arthur W. Pink, *The Sovereignty of God* (London, England: Banner of Truth, 1968), 70.

[282] Sproul, *Chosen by God*, 72-73.

[283] Qtd in Allen and Lemke, *Whosoever Will*, 138.

John Piper expressed it like this:

> New birth is a miraculous creation of God that
> enables a formerly "dead" person to receive Christ
> and so be saved. We do not bring about the new
> birth by our faith. God brings about our faith by
> the new birth.[284]

So, plainly, a principal part of Calvinism is the belief that we
are born again before we can believe the gospel. Many Christians
will likely find this doctrine of Calvinism to be unique and a classic
case of getting the cart before the horse. It seems to fly in the face of
the clear scriptural teaching that we must believe in Jesus Christ in
order to have eternal life (John 3:14,15). When the Philippian jailer
was convicted and asked Paul what he needed to do to be saved,
Paul responded, "Believe on the Lord Jesus Christ, and thou shalt
be saved, and thy house" (Acts 16:31). If the Calvinistic position
were true, Paul's statement is dishonest, and he should have replied,
"There is nothing you can do to be saved, unless God decides to
regenerate you with his sovereign grace. Then, if he chooses to
do so, you will believe on him, in which case your believing isn't
the *cause* of salvation; it's actually the *evidence* of salvation." Paul,
however, does not espouse Calvinism, so he unashamedly declares
that the jailer of Philippi must believe in Christ to be saved. Norman
Geisler's comment is apropos: "Never does the Bible say, 'Be saved
in order to believe'; instead, repeatedly, it commands, 'Believe in
order to be saved.'"[285]

But, let's not get too far ahead of ourselves! We must look at *why*
Calvinists maintain that regeneration precedes faith. It is essential to
grasp what Calvinism teaches in order to comprehend why they assert
that regeneration must precede faith and to satisfactorily respond

---

[284] Accessed at https://www.desiringgod.org/articles/what-we-believe-
about-the-five-points-of-calvinism#Grace
[285] Norman Geisler, *Systematic Theology in One Volume* (Minneapolis, MN:
Bethany House, 2011), 774.

to their argumentation. Once we have observed carefully their argument, we will examine it and discover that it is an inadequate interpretation of the Bible and that it serves as a tremendous threat to the church of Jesus Christ.

An Explanation of the Calvinistic Perspective

So, why do Calvinists insist that regeneration must precede faith? The answer lies in their view of fallen man's condition.[286] Men and women are born "dead in trespasses and sins" (Ephesians 2:1). Unregenerate people do not have the ability to respond positively to God's gracious invitations. They are dead, like a corpse, and will no more receive Christ than a dead dog would go fetch his bone. For the Calvinist, to be dead spiritually is to be without the capacity to receive the gospel. The words of R. C. Sproul are a good representation of the Calvinists' position: "In order for one who is dead to the things of God to come alive to God, something must be done to him and for him. Dead men cannot make themselves come alive. Dead men cannot create spiritual life within themselves."[287]

To strengthen his point, Sproul recounts a common illustration that preachers use in evangelism to get sinners to see their desperate need of Christ. He describes the plight of a man who is about to drown in the sea:

---

[286] Their view of fallen man is known as total depravity. What Calvinists mean by total depravity is expressed in the Westminster Confession of Faith (Chapter 9, Section 3): "Man, by his fall into a state of sin, hath wholly lost all ability of will to any spiritual good accompanying salvation: so as, a natural man, being altogether averse from that good, and dead in sin, is not able, by his own strength, to convert himself, or to prepare himself thereunto." Unregenerate sinners, in Calvinism, not only cannot earn their own salvation (every Christian ought to agree with this position), but cannot even accept God's free gift of salvation in the gospel.

[287] Sproul, *Chosen by God*, 114.

In this view fallen man is seen as a drowning man who is unable to swim. He has gone under twice and bobbed to the surface for the last time. If he goes under again he will die. His only hope is for God to throw him a life preserver. God throws the lifeline and tosses it precisely to the edge of the man's outstretched fingers. All the man has to do to be saved is to grab hold. If he will only grab hold of the life preserver, God will tow him in. If he refuses the life preserver, he will certainly perish.[288]

What is wrong with this illustration? To Sproul, it rightly describes man's utter helplessness, but it fails to address adequately Paul's description of fallen man as being dead in his sins. He isn't merely drowning in his sins, soon to perish in an ocean of sinful despair; instead, he is lifeless at the bottom of the ocean and will remain dead unless God chooses to impart spiritual life. According to the Calvinist, this is what spiritual death means. To be spiritually dead is to be unresponsive in relation to God.

Based on this understanding of spiritual death, Calvinists proceed to argue that no person has the capacity to receive the gospel. To support this argument, they typically appeal to a few scattered passages. Jesus, for example, declared, "No man can come to me, except the Father which hath sent me draw him: and I will raise him up at the last day" (John 6:44).[289] Then, Paul insisted that "the carnal mind is enmity against God: for it is not subject to the law of God, neither indeed can be. So then they that are in the flesh cannot please God" (Romans 8:7,8). He also reasoned that "the natural man receiveth not the things of the Spirit of God: for they are foolishness unto him: neither can he know them, because they are spiritually discerned" (1 Corinthians 2:14). This flurry of verses is usually followed by an explanation that nobody has the moral ability to come to Christ, to please God, or to receive the gospel because our

---

[288] Ibid., 116.

[289] This verse was addressed in the chapter on John 6.

natural condition as fallen human beings leads us to abhor the idea of the God of the Bible.

To a Calvinist, the reason why no natural person receives Christ is because he does not want to receive Christ. In his natural state, he hates God, fleeing from his presence and daring to defy his commands. After all, Paul, in quoting the Old Testament, wrote, "There is none righteous, no, not one: there is none that understandeth, there is none that seeketh after God. They are all gone out of the way, they are together become unprofitable; there is none that doeth good, no, not one" (Romans 3:10-12). Apparently, no one, apart from regeneration, has ever sought God. Once God brings a person to life, he will seek after God and find Christ. Jen Wilkin, in her book *None Like Him*, espouses this viewpoint: "In our fallen sinful state, we are unwilling to come to him. So God regenerates us, changing the disposition of our hearts. Then, from our own will, which is finally freed from its bondage, we willingly respond to his call to come to him and be saved."[290]

So, accordingly, we come into this world dead in our sins and trespasses, without the capacity to do any spiritual good, blind to the truth of the gospel, enslaved to the desires of our sinful flesh, and incapable of coming to Christ. According to the Calvinist, the only way that we can have eternal life, do spiritual good, receive the gospel, and be free from our bondage to sin is if God sovereignly regenerates us. After all, Jesus did tell Nicodemus that "except a man be born again, he cannot see the kingdom of God" (John 3:3). Unless we are born again, we will remain in our transgressions until the day we die.

An Examination of Calvinistic Proof-texts

Upon initial inspection, the Calvinistic description of fallen man appears to rest on a solid biblical foundation. If Calvinism is correct in its assessment of man's depravity, then their account of pre-faith

---

[290] Jen Wilkin, *None Like Him* (Wheaton: Crossway, 2016), 145.

regeneration would seem to be a necessary logical implication. Let's not accept their account of man's sinful condition, however, without a careful investigation into the verses often employed to build their doctrine. Too many men have accepted blindly the Calvinists' teaching without listening to other theological voices. Presuppositions are powerful, and once a person puts on the Calvinists' glasses, he is hindered from objectively evaluating the position in order to determine whether it is biblical.

The first question that must be asked is this: Does the Bible equate spiritual death with physical death? It doesn't take too long to discover that Calvinists insist that spiritual death is corpse-like death. To be dead spiritually is to be like a physically dead person, incapable of responding to external stimuli. This Calvinistic assumption runs throughout their literature, but is there biblical warrant for such a position? Or is spiritual death described differently in the Scriptures?

For certain, spiritual death is the consequence of sin. At the very beginning of human history, God commanded Adam, "Of every tree of the garden thou mayest freely eat: but of the tree of the knowledge of good and evil, thou shalt not eat of it: for *in the day that thou eatest thereof thou shalt surely die*" (Genesis 2:16,17). Adam and Eve were presented with a choice to either obey or disobey the command of God. They could have refrained from eating of the fruit from the tree of the knowledge of good and evil. As Marston and Forster write, "Nothing in the Bible hints that the first human's wrong choice might have been the will of God."[291] Why they chose to disobey is certainly a mystery, but the consequence of their sinful behavior was immediate spiritual death, just as God had declared.

But, what is spiritual death? Several theologians and commentators define spiritual death as separation from God. Norman Geisler maintains that spiritual death "does not mean a total destruction of all ability to hear and respond to God but a complete separation of the whole person from God."[292] David Allen concurs, "Spiritual death means separation from God, not a total

---

[291] Marston and Forster, *God's Strategy in Human History*, 34.

[292] Geisler, *Chosen But Free*, 63.

destruction of all ability to hear and respond to God."[293] This is consistent with the conclusion of Allen Ross: "The basic idea [of spiritual death] seems to be more of alienation or separation rather than cessation or annihilation."[294] Each of these brilliant Christian thinkers agrees that to be spiritually dead is to be alienated from a relationship with God, not to be as unresponsive as a corpse.

This seems to describe the situation of Adam after he disobeyed God's command. After all, as John Lennox observes, "Since Adam was the one who committed that sin, he is by definition the paradigm case of what it means to be dead in trespasses and sins."[295] Upon partaking of the fruit in direct disobedience to God, he died spiritually. In this condition, however, Adam still possessed the capacity to hear God calling to him (Genesis 3:9,10). If Calvinism's description of spiritual death was accurate, then "Adam should not have been able to hear God's voice and respond to him."[296] The fact that Adam could respond to God's gracious initiative should inform us that something is amiss in the Calvinistic account of what it means to be spiritually dead.

A flaw, then, in the argument for regeneration preceding faith is that "it is based on an unbiblical analogy involving *physical death*."[297] There is no biblical justification for equating spiritual death with physical death. Throughout the Bible, spiritual death is represented as humanity's rebellion and separation from God. This can be seen clearly in the famous story of the Prodigal Son (Luke 15:11-32). One of the father's sons demanded his inheritance, left the father's house, wasted his money on sinful living, reached rock bottom, and returned back home. His father warmly embraced him, forgave him, and celebrated by throwing a huge party. The most important

---

[293] David L. Allen, "Does Regeneration Precede Faith?" *JBTM* 11:2 (2014): 34-52.

[294] Allen Ross, *Creation & Blessing* (Grand Rapids, MI: Baker Academic, 1997), 125.

[295] Lennox, *Determined to Believe?*, 155.

[296] Ibid., 160.

[297] Ibid., 163. Italics his.

part, though, for our current discussion is how the father depicted his rebellious son's lost condition. He declared, "For this my son was *dead*, and *is alive again*; he was lost, and is found" (Luke 15:24; also verse 32). Just as this prodigal son was "dead" because of his separation from his father, likewise sinful people are spiritually dead because they are "lost" and alienated from God.

So, we have observed what exactly spiritual death means according to the Scriptures. It is metaphorical of our separation from God, not a corpse-like inability to receive the gospel. Moreover, the Calvinistic explanation of spiritual death is problematic for a number of other reasons. For one thing, although Calvinists insist that to be dead means that we cannot respond positively to God, they argue that sinful people willingly reject the gospel. In his book *The Potter's Freedom*, James White argues, "Unregenerate men who are enemies of God most assuredly respond to God: in a universally negative fashion. They are constantly suppressing the knowledge of God that is within their hearts, so it is simply untrue to assert they do not respond to God. They respond in rebellion and sinfulness, but respond they do!"[298] However, this makes little sense if spiritual death is equated with physical death. Surely, if we are dead like a corpse, we will never receive the gospel unless we are made alive, but neither will we reject the gospel.[299] A corpse certainly cannot respond positively to a command to take out the trash, but neither can it reject a command to take out the trash. It is rather inconsistent to take an imbalanced interpretation of an obvious analogy that describes our sinful separation from God.

Another problem with misunderstanding spiritual death to be like physical death is the inconsistency that arises in explaining why Christians sin. The New Testament teaches that it is possible for born-again believers to sin against God. While sin does not have dominion over them, it is a possibility that should be avoided and carefully guarded against. Paul encouraged believers in Rome to

---

[298] James White, *The Potter's Freedom* (Calvary Publishing Press, 2009), 98.
[299] Dave Hunt, *What Love Is This?* (Bend, OR: The Berean Call, 2013), 151. He writes, "Neither can a dead man reject Christ, nor can he even sin."

consider themselves dead to sin (Romans 6:11), presumably because those who receive Christ by faith partake of his death. Now, the question for the Calvinist to answer is this: If *dead in sins* (Ephesians 2:1) means an inability to respond positively to God, why doesn't *dead to sin* (Romans 6:11) mean an inability, for the believer, to respond positively to sin?[300] It is arbitrary to take the analogy very woodenly in the first case but very loosely in the second case.

A final argument against the Calvinistic notion of spiritual death is that this is not the only metaphor used in the Bible to describe our sinful condition. Jesus, for instance, employed the analogy of people that are physically sick: "They that are whole have no need of the physician, but they that are sick: I came not to call the righteous, but sinners to repentance" (Mark 2:17). Furthermore, Paul wrote to Titus that Jesus had died in order to "purify unto himself a peculiar people" (Titus 2:14), implying that these people were in need of purification. Geisler's assessment of these analogies is correct: "Clearly a sick person is able to receive a cure, just as a dirty person can embrace cleansing."[301] Likewise, spiritually dead people can believe the gospel, just as Jesus declared that "the dead shall hear the voice of the Son of God: and they that hear shall live" (John 5:25).

Calvinists have assumed, perhaps subconsciously, that there is direct parallel between spiritual death and physical death. John MacArthur, for example, in a sermon entitled "Coming Alive in Christ," commits this fundamental error:

> The best way to see [spiritual death] is in reference to physical death. Physical death is an inability to respond, no matter what the stimulus is. Physical death means you can't react. You've been to enough funerals and so have I to know what physical death is. It doesn't matter what the stimulus is, no ...

---

[300] The inspiration for this point comes from Leighton Flowers: https://soteriology101.com/2018/04/13/born-dead/.

[301] Geisler, *Systematic Theology in One Volume*, 772.

no physically dead individual ever reacts to any stimulus.

He continued:

> Spiritual death is the same thing. All the caresses and all of the affection and all the tears and the love of God draw out absolutely nothing. Because a spiritually dead person is alienated from the life of God. There is no capacity for a response.[302]

This is an unfortunate case of "theological misinterpretation arising from the use of an unbiblical and, in fact, irrelevant analogy."[303] Calvinists should not presuppose that spiritual death closely resembles physical death without the Scripture's permission. Sadly, those who adhere to Calvinism "tend to equate spiritual deadness with physical deadness and do not qualify this spiritual deadness in the light of other descriptions of lostness."[304] The consequence of this hermeneutical error is that Calvinists create an entire theological system based on the false premise that individuals are born without the ability to receive the saving grace of Jesus Christ. Once this faulty explanation of spiritual deadness is exposed, then the rest of Calvinistic soteriology is undermined.

What about the other passages that Calvinists use to teach total inability? Since we have been investigating a passage in one of Paul's letters (Ephesians), let's tackle a couple of the other passages in Paul's writings. Again, he wrote in 1 Corinthians that "the natural man receiveth not the things of the Spirit of God: for they are foolishness unto him: neither can he know them, because they are spiritually discerned" (2:14). What's the problem with the Calvinistic

---

[302] John MacArthur, "Coming Alive in Christ," available online at https://www.gty.org/library/sermons-library/1908/coming-alive-in-christ.

[303] Lennox, *Determined to Believe?*, 162.

[304] Allen and Lemke, *Whosoever Will*, 135.

interpretation? After all, the text does clearly say that an unsaved person doesn't receive the Spirit of God.

Actually ... Read the passage again. Paul says that the natural person doesn't receive "the things of the Spirit of God." There is a big difference between not being able to receive the things of the Spirit and not being able to receive the Spirit. Paul is clarifying in 1 Corinthians 2:14 that an unsaved person will not be able to comprehend the spiritual things of God, because they are spiritually discerned. Leon Morris is accurate, "Anyone whose equipment is only of this world, who has not received the Holy Spirit, has no ability to make an estimate of things spiritual."[305] God reveals spiritual things by the Spirit, so anyone without the Spirit will be unable to accept and grasp them. This verse is completely irrelevant in establishing a doctrine of total inability, since it does not address who is able to receive the gospel.

Paul's bold assertion in Romans 8:8 that those who "are in the flesh cannot please God" is often employed by Calvinists to imply that unbelievers cannot believe the gospel. White writes, "The lost man *cannot please God*. Is repentance and faith pleasing to God? Yes. Is submission to the commands of God pleasing to Him? Of course. Therefore, regeneration must take place first."[306] The argument by advocates of Calvinism is simple:

1. Those who are in the flesh cannot please God.
2. Believing the gospel is pleasing to God.
3. Therefore, those who are in the flesh cannot believe the gospel.

Is this argument correct? No. Paul is simply teaching that no one who lives in obedience to his fleshly desires can be pleasing to God. No unsaved person can perfectly submit to God's law and obey it. But the fact that unsaved people cannot live in obedience

---

[305] Leon Morris, *Tyndale New Testament Commentaries- 1 Corinthians* (Grand Rapids, MI: Wm. B. Eerdmans Publishing, 1987), 59.
[306] White, *The Potter's Freedom*, 84. Italics his.

to God does not mean that unsaved people cannot believe in Jesus Christ. Leighton Flowers, on his tremendous website revealing the errors of Calvinism (Soteriology 101), makes this point, "Mankind's inability to submit to God's law does not prove their inability to trust in Christ who fulfilled the law for mankind. Mankind's inability to please God while acting in the flesh does not prove mankind's inability to respond to the spiritual appeal of God."[307] Therefore, as A. T. Robertson wrote, "This does not mean that the sinner has no responsibility and cannot be saved. He is responsible and can be saved by the change of heart through the Holy Spirit."[308]

Finally, Calvinists often stress Paul's stern statement that "there is none that seeketh after God" (Romans 3:11). They interpret this passage very literally. Apparently, no unregenerate person has ever sought God apart from an irresistible, effectual work of grace in his heart by the Holy Spirit, after which he is enabled to seek God. This, however, would seem to contradict other passages of Scripture that reveal unsaved people seeking God: "[God] hath made of one blood all nations of men for to dwell on all the face of the earth, and hath determined the times before appointed, and the bounds of their habitation; *that they should seek the Lord*, if haply they might feel after him, and find him, though he be not far from every one of us" (Acts 17:26,27). Robert Shank explains the error of the Calvinistic reading of Romans 3:

> Failure to recognize hyperbole, a frequent device in Biblical literature, has involved many in an erroneous definition of human depravity that makes God's appeals and exhortations ludicrous, if not shamefully insincere … In Psalm 14, from which Paul quotes in Romans 3, David asserts that none seeks after God; but he also speaks of God's people, whom the non-seekers oppress, and of those

---

[307] Accessed at https://soteriology101.com/2016/03/16/answering-cal vinistic-proof-texts/.
[308] Robertson, *Word Pictures in the New Testament- Vol. IV*, 373.

for whom the Lord is a refuge. It is obvious that non-seeking was not universal in David's day, despite his hyperbolic assertion, and the Scriptures witness that in every generation some have sought God, who always has had His remnant."[309]

In the end, the doctrine of total depravity as defined by Calvinists is a doctrine in search of a verse. If this doctrine crumbles, then sinful humans, although fallen and spiritually dead (Ephesians 2:1), can receive God's gracious invitation. The plain sense of Scripture indicates that anyone can be saved by believing in Jesus Christ.

The Clear *Ordo Salutis* in Scripture

The Latin phrase *ordo salutis* is an expression that simply means the "order of salvation." As has been seen in this chapter, Calvinism insists on a unique *ordo salutis* that places regeneration before faith. This, again, is a shock to many people, since not one verse in the entire Bible says that regeneration precedes faith, and it would appear that the Scriptures teach the exact opposite. However, there is a reason for why Calvinists subscribe to pre-faith regeneration. Because of their interpretation of spiritual death, adherents of Calvinistic theology contend that God must bring people to spiritual life before they can believe. Again, according to R. C. Sproul, "We do not believe in order to be born again; we are born again in order that we may believe."[310]

Many students of the Bible reach a different conclusion concerning the order of salvation. Without the contaminating presuppositions of Calvinism, most people will interpret the Scriptures to teach that sinners receive eternal life, are born again, and inherit salvation by believing on the Lord Jesus Christ. God desires everyone to be saved (1 Timothy 2:4) and has provided salvation for the sins of the whole

---

[309] Shank, *Elect in the Son*, 205.
[310] Sproul, *Chosen by God*, 73.

world through the atoning work of Jesus Christ (1 John 2:2). However, he will not force anyone to be saved against his wishes. He convicts the world (John 16:8) and draws all people to himself (John 12:32), but he saves only when the condition of faith and repentance is met. Once a sinner surrenders his life to God and receives the free gift of salvation, God saves him, gives him new life (regeneration), adopts him into his family, and declares him righteous. None of these activities of God, including regeneration, occurs prior to a sinner's faith.

To show that this is the clear, biblical *ordo salutis*, we will quickly look at *four* different passages found in John's Gospel that specifically address this topic. Before looking at these passages, it's important to correct an oft-repeated criticism of the perspective espoused in this chapter. Some Calvinists accuse non-Calvinists of self-salvation. That is, non-Calvinists apparently believe that people have the ability to regenerate themselves. Loraine Boettner, for instance, is guilty of this fallacious accusation in his book *The Reformed Doctrine of Predestination*. He criticizes non-Calvinists by asserting that "man does not possess the power of *self-regeneration*."[311] For him, the capacity to believe the gospel implies that people regenerate themselves. In other words, Boettner wants to show that those who do not hold to Calvinism actually believe that they can save themselves.

Two things must be said in response to this allegation. First, no non-Calvinist, to my knowledge, accepts that sinful people regenerate themselves. God is the one who saves, regenerates, adopts, justifies, sanctifies, and glorifies. However- *and this must be emphasized*- he only regenerates when the condition of faith and repentance is met. Our responsibility is to believe the gospel. In response to our repentant faith, God regenerates us. Certainly, as Boettner insists, no man has "the power of self-regeneration," but this does not suggest that he cannot be regenerated by receiving Christ.

Second, it should not be forgotten that man, in a sense, saves himself and is thus his own savior.[312] We cannot, of course, save

---

[311] Loraine Boettner, *The Reformed Doctrine of Predestination* (Phillipsburg, NJ: Presbyterian and Reformed Publishing Company, 1932), 68. Italics mine.
[312] Shank, *Life in the Son*, 96.

ourselves through our good works, but we can save ourselves by trusting in the gospel of Jesus Christ. After all, Peter testified to a large crowd about the death and resurrection of the Messiah, exhorting them to "save [themselves] from this untoward generation" (Acts 2:40). Furthermore, Paul wrote to his young son in the faith Timothy to "take heed unto thyself, and unto the doctrine; continue in them: for in doing this thou shalt both *save* thyself, and them that hear thee" (1 Timothy 4:16). During his earthly ministry, Jesus describes the demands of discipleship: "Whosoever will save his life shall lose it; but whosoever shall lose his life for my sake and the gospel's, *the same shall save it*" (Mark 8:35). The Calvinistic charge that non-Calvinists believe in "self-regeneration" is both false (since God is the one regenerates on the basis of faith and repentance) and misguided (since the Bible encourages individuals to save themselves by trusting in the gospel).

Now, let's look at the clear *ordo salutis* found throughout John's Gospel. Here are four passages that clearly teach that faith comes before regeneration:

> He came unto his own, and his own received him not. But as many as received him, to them gave he power to become the sons of God, even to them that believe on his name: which were born, not of blood, nor of the will of the flesh, nor of the will of man, but of God (John 1:11-13).

> And as Moses lifted up the serpent in the wilderness, even so must the Son of man be lifted up: that whosoever believeth in him should not perish, but have eternal life (John 3:14,15).

> Jesus said unto her, I am the resurrection, and the life: he that believeth in me, though he were dead, yet shall he live (John 11:25).

And many other signs truly did Jesus in the presence
of his disciples, which are not written in this book:
but these are written, that ye might believe that Jesus
is the Christ, the Son of God; and that believing ye
might have life through his name (John 20:30,31).

Related Issues

There are three other difficulties that relate to the Calvinistic
position of pre-faith regeneration. For starters, it diminishes the need
for apologetics in preaching, evangelism, and missions. Apologetics
deals with reasonable defenses of the faith against opposing attacks
and usually involves the topics of God's existence, the resurrection of
Jesus Christ, and the trustworthiness of the Bible. Preachers, pastors,
and missionaries often use apologetics to persuade people to believe
in Jesus Christ. This certainly was the methodology employed by the
Apostle Paul, as can be seen in the last chapter of the book of Acts:

And when they had appointed him a day, there
came many to him into his lodging; to whom he
expounded and testified the kingdom of God,
persuading them concerning Jesus, both out of the the
law of Moses, and out of the prophets, from morning
till evening. And some believed the things which
were spoken, and some believed not (Acts 28:23,24).

So Paul, and presumably the other early Christians, argued
passionately to convince sinners that Jesus is the Christ, has died for
the sins of the world, and has risen from the dead to authenticate his
salvific mission. He didn't just throw out the gospel and let the chips
fall where they landed; instead, he persuaded them "from morning
till evening." It appears that Paul thought his efforts could actually
lead to the salvation of those that he was persuading.

But, if Calvinism is true, why did the Apostle Paul argue with
unbelievers in Acts 28? Or, to ask it more broadly, what is the use

of persuasion in any evangelistic setting? If sinners do not have the ability to freely receive the gospel without regeneration, then wouldn't it be useless and illogical to attempt to persuade a sinner that Christianity is true? If spiritual death implies a corpse-like inability to respond positively to God's grace, then persuasion is a waste of time, because the unregenerate person will never, ever believe the message of Christ until God, if he so chooses, regenerates him. Surely, many Calvinists will reply to this quandary like R. C. Sproul: "God not only foreordains the *end* of salvation for the elect, he also foreordained the *means* to that end."[313] This, however, is not a satisfactory response but a lousy assertion that fails to address the issue. Attempting to convince ungenerate men and women about the truth of Christianity would result in abysmal failure every time. Nevertheless, just like the Apostle Paul's ministry, it does seem that apologetics has proven to be a useful tool in persuading people to believe in Jesus Christ.

A second additional conundrum is that it fails to address the biblical teaching of men rejecting God's will for their lives. One interesting passage is found in Luke's Gospel, and it specifically states that certain people rejected God's plan for them:

> And all the people that heard him, and the publicans, justified God, being baptized with the baptism of John. But the Pharisees and lawyers rejected the counsel of God against themselves, being not baptized of him (Luke 7:29,30).

God's plan for the Pharisees and lawyers was that they should experience the baptism of John. They, however, refused his plan for themselves, not because God had determined that they should reject it, but because they willingly chose to reject John's baptism. This observation should be balanced, though, with the steadfast belief that human beings cannot "thwart God's ultimate plan for

---

[313] Sproul, *Chosen by God*, 210. Italics his.

the world," even though they can individually opt out of his will for their lives.[314]

Another passage that demonstrates that grace is not irresistible is the story of the rich young ruler (Luke 18:18-23). At the conclusion of this sad story, which involves the rich young ruler refusing to sell his goods and follow Christ, Jesus declares:

> How hardly shall they that have riches enter into the kingdom of God! For it is easier for a camel to go through a needle's eye, than for a rich man to enter into the kingdom of God (Luke 18:24,25).

Doesn't this, though, contradict the Calvinists' claim that regeneration is irresistible? Steve Lemke powerfully argues that it does. He writes:

> If Jesus were a Calvinist, He never would have suggested that it was harder for rich persons to be saved by God's irresistible grace than a poor person. Their wills would be changed immediately and invincibly upon hearing God's effectual call. It would be no harder for a rich person to be saved by God's monergistic and irresistible calling than it would be for any other sinner. But the real Jesus was suggesting that their salvation was tied in some measure to their response and commitment to His calling.[315]

Lemke is exactly right, and many other Scriptures support his conclusion that saving grace can be resisted by a person. Stephen told those who were murdering him that they always resisted the Holy Ghost (Acts 7:51); God had said through the prophet Isaiah that he had held out his hands all day long to a disobedient and obstinate

---

[314] Marston and Forster, *God's Strategy in Human History*, 110.

[315] Allen and Lemke, *Whosoever Will*, 120-121.

people (Romans 10:21); and Jesus mourned over the inhabitants of Jerusalem because he longed to gather their children together, but they were not willing (Matthew 23:37). Each of these instances is a mockery if Calvinism is true, since God was withholding the necessary grace for the people to do what they should have done and then complaining about their actions, even though they *literally* could not have done any other than what they were doing.[316]

Finally, Calvinism's account of pre-faith regeneration treats us as robots, not as persons. It seems rather commonsensical that "personal relationships require mutuality."[317] Roger Olson, in his book *Against Calvinism*, raises this critique:

> Common sense alone dictates that a truly personal relationship always involves free will; insofar as one party controls the other such that the other has no real choice whether to be in the relationship or not, it is not a real relationship.[318]

This is surely true in human relationships, so there is no reason to believe that it would change in our relationship with God. Vincent Brummer, a Dutch philosopher and theologian, defends this notion of mutuality in our personal relationship with God. He notes:

> A personal relationship with God assumes that the human partner also remains a person in the relationship and that his or her free choice is equally a necessary condition for the relationship to be brought about ... God cannot bring about our choice without it ceasing to be ours. By definition, a personal relationship with God cannot be factually unavoidable for the human partner. For this reason the doctrine of factual irresistibility excludes a

---

[316] See chapter "Is Free Will for Real?" for a discussion on what free will is.
[317] Olson, *Against Calvinism*, 167.
[318] Ibid., 168.

personal relationship between God and human persons.[319]

Calvinism denies the importance of our choice to enter into the relationship God desires for us. God earnestly pursues our salvation and patiently woos us with his grace, love, and merciful longsuffering. However, he will not make the choice for us to receive this grace. By faith, we must appropriate all that God offers us in the gospel. For God to irresistibly change us so that we will necessarily come to Christ is to eliminate and exclude the personal aspect of our relationship with him. It diminishes us to puppets who are manipulated by God to choose him. It removes the prerequisite necessary to any healthy relationship: "mutual, informed consent."[320]

---

[319] Qtd in Ibid., 168.
[320] Ibid.

PART 3

The Practical Problems of Calvinism

CHAPTER 8

Assurance and Perseverance

There is no knowledge in the universe nearly as important as knowing that you are saved. Equally true is the fact that nothing is more deadly and dangerous than a person having a false assurance of his salvation. Assured that his eternal destiny is secure, he lives his life without the knowledge that he is headed to a Christ-less eternity. However, for the believer, possessing genuine assurance of eternal life empowers him to suffer for the cause of Christ, face the challenges thrown his way, and fight for the truth of God's word. The Christian who does not possess this blessed assurance will be plagued by constant anxiety, which will inevitably hinder his spiritual growth and effectiveness.

Fortunately, God desires for his people to know that they are saved. He does not reserve this knowledge for a special class of elite Christians. On the contrary, as John Miley asserted, "The comfortable assurance of a gracious sonship is a common Christian privilege."[321] It is a universal birthright granted to the children of God. While the depth of this assurance might vary during the Christian life, dependent upon our experiences and

---

[321] Miley, *Systematic Theology- Volume II*, 352.

level of commitment to Christ, no believer is prevented from a full knowledge of salvation.

The Scriptures support this assertion. For instance, Paul wrote, "Because ye are sons, God hath sent forth the Spirit of his Son into your hearts, crying, Abba, Father" (Galatians 4:6). Notice that he did not offer remarkable qualifications, such as age or position in the church, for the working of the Spirit in our hearts to cry out in adoration to God. Instead, it was simply the reality of sonship.

Undoubtedly, then, God wants his church to receive the knowledge of the truth that their sins are forgiven and that they are heirs of eternal life. As a matter of fact, John penned his first letter, in part, in order that his readers might know that they are saved: "These things have I written unto you that believe on the name of the Son of God; *that ye may know that ye have eternal life*" (1 John 5:13). It would be deceitful on the part of God to withhold this valuable assurance from those who believe on the Lord Jesus Christ.

But, how can Christians know that they are saved? It is easier to assert the reality of assurance than it is to explain the manner in which it seems to operate in individual believers. Some theologians argue that there are two distinct witnesses who jointly testify to the status of our souls. Both are equally important and scriptural.

How to Know That You're Saved

The first is the witness of the Spirit. The Spirit testifies to our hearts that we belong to the family of God. Paul confirmed this when he wrote that "*the Spirit itself beareth witness* with our spirit, that we are the children of God" (Romans 8:16). This testimony "consists in a communication made by the Holy Spirit to the believer's mind of the fact that his sins are forgiven, that he is reconciled to God, and that the filial relation, which was destroyed by disobedience, is now restored by grace through faith."[322] Importantly, this witness of the

---

[322] Richard Taylor, *Leading Wesleyan Thinkers- Volume 3* (Kansas City, MI: Beacon Hill Press), 176.

Spirit cannot occur in an *unbeliever's* life. This work is performed in the consciousness of believers after adoption, not before adoption (Galatians 4:6). Assurance comes to Christians, not before conversion or during conversion, but after conversion, by an operation of the Spirit who assures us that we are children of the King.

The second witness is that of ourselves. As we follow Christ and obey his commandments, we are a witness to ourselves that we are saved. This, of course, requires a certain level of introspection. Examining his own life, a Christian will see signs of a genuine conversion. But, what signs can a believer see that will give him assurance? Remember that John wrote 1 John to assist the body of Christ in gaining assurance of their salvation. He provides a few important ways for Christians to know that they possess eternal life.

First, there is valid assurance only for those whose faith is in Christ Jesus. It is necessary to note that John did *not* say that he wrote "these things" so everyone can know that they have eternal life. He qualified his statement by limiting it to those who "believe on the name of the Son of God" (1 John 5:13). Just as salvation can be found in "no other name under heaven" (Acts 4:12), except the precious name of Jesus, authentic assurance cannot be experienced by anyone apart from a saving relationship with the "Savior of the world" (1 John 4:14).

Second, John provides another evidence of salvation: "Hereby we do know that we know him, if we keep his commandments. He that saith, I know him, and keepeth not his commandments, is a liar, and the truth is not in him" (1 John 2:3,4). A Christian demonstrates the validity of his salvation by faithfully obeying the commandments of Jesus. Obviously, obedience to Christ's words does not merit or earn eternal life. However, it does serve as an undeniable proof that we have been transformed by God's saving grace. Fortunately, John does not leave us in doubt as to whether we are walking in the truth. If you are *not* committed to keeping the commandments of Jesus Christ, then you are not a Christian and consequently have no assurance of eternal life.

A third and final way to know that you are a true believer is whether you love the people of God. John wrote, "We know that have passed from death to life, because we love the brethren" (1 John 3:14). It seems that several people live by the mantra of "I love Christ, but not his church." According to John, that is an impossibility. Granted, it is understandable why a person would claim to be in love with Jesus while failing to participate in a local church. The nasty attitudes and actions of many "Christians" has put a bad taste in some people's mouth. However, it is just as sinful for a person to refuse to participate in a local church as it is for those in the church to treat other people horribly. A tell-tale indicator of our spiritual rebirth is our affection for God's people.

So, let's conduct a brief self-examination. Is your faith solely and completely in the Son of God and his finished work? Are you endeavoring to walk as he walked? Do you care for your brothers and sisters in Christ? If your response to these questions is in the affirmative, you can know that you have eternal life. You can be assured of your eternal destiny.

How Does This Relate to Calvinism?

Great! I'm glad that I can know that I'm right with the Lord. I already knew that, though! So, why are you still writing? The aim of this book has been to provide a thoughtful critique of Calvinistic soteriology. It is my contention that, *carried to its logical conclusion, Calvinism hinders Christians from actually knowing whether they are saved.* The reasoning for this bold assertion is how Calvinists describe the nature of saving faith and explain those who "depart from the faith" (1 Timothy 4:1).

For Calvinists, the faith that truly saves is a faith that endures to the end. A person who professes the Christian faith for a time, only to eventually fall away, was never saved in the first place. His conversion was counterfeit. The elect, chosen by God before the foundation of the world and effectually drawn by the Spirit at God's appointed time and place, will necessarily persevere to the end. Anyone who does not persevere to the end of his life demonstrates that he was never saved, regardless of whatever good works he might have accomplished in the name of Christ.

In his book *Stop Asking Jesus into Your Heart*, J. D. Greear articulates this position. He writes, "Saving faith always endures to the end ... Since those who are truly saved can never lose it, we must conclude that a failure to heed the warnings demonstrates that we never possessed true saving faith to begin with."[323] Later, he provides an alliterated expression that summarizes the Calvinistic viewpoint: "Faith that fizzles before the finish was flawed from the first."[324] Greear is not ambiguous in his book; if you fall away from the faith before cross the finish line, you were never in the race. You were a pretender, an imposter, in spite of how zealous your obedience for Christ might have been.

Influential Calvinist R. C. Sproul agreed with this perspective. In his work *What Is Reformed Theology?* he observed, "We have all known people who have made professions of faith and exhibited zeal for Christ, only to repudiate their confessions and turn away from Christ."[325] Because Calvinistic soteriology does not allow for true believers to apostatize, how should Calvinists respond to these situations? One reason for this departure from the faith is that "their profession was not genuine in the first place."[326] Had their profession been genuine, they would have inevitably endured until the end.

So, it's important to grasp what most Calvinists actually believe in order for this argument to be effective. Of course, there is no doubt that some people have false conversions. For instance, 1 John 2:19 states, "They went out from us, but they were not of us; for if they had been of us, they would no doubt have continued with us." Calvinists love to quote this verse to support their contention that

---

[323] J. D. Greear, *Stop Asking Jesus into Your Heart* (Nashville, TN: B&H Academic, 2013), 79.

[324] Ibid., 87.

[325] Sproul, *What is Reformed Theology?*, 208.

[326] Ibid.

those who depart from the Christian faith were not truly saved.[327] However, it seems unscriptural to maintain that everyone who walks away from Christ had never been saved. Shank's advice is helpful:

> John was writing of specific instances, rather than stating a universal principle. Let us beware the fallacy of assuming that all truth can and must be compressed into a single sentence of Scripture, and that the precise circumstance in one instance of defection necessarily governs the circumstance in all other instances. There are some whose professions of faith are false from the beginning, and there are others who abandon faith and withdraw from a saving relationship with Christ. The Scriptures recognize both circumstances, and the precise circumstance of the antichrists cited by John determines nothing with respect to the circumstance in other instances.[328]

Here is Calvinistic thinking, then, in a nutshell: Those who professed the faith but eventually fell away didn't actually possess the faith. You might say, "Well, that doesn't seem to be much of a problem." I believe you are wrong. My questions for the Calvinist are simple. Did those who fell away from the faith think that they were saved? Had they deceived not only others but also themselves? In their own judgment, did they, at the time of their profession, consider themselves to be in the family of God? Some Calvinistic authors appear to affirm that the reprobate can experience a measure of God's grace to such a degree that they feel like they are elect.

---

[327] They also cite Matthew 7:23, where Jesus instructs that he will say to some who have "cast out devils" and "done many wonderful works": "I never knew you."

[328] Shank, *Life in the Son*, 362.

John Calvin, in an effort to salvage his beloved theological system from destruction, asserted that "experience shows that the reprobate are sometimes affected in a way so similar to the elect, that even *in their own judgment* there is no difference between them."[329] In the same paragraph, he writes, "There is nothing to prevent an inferior operation of the Spirit from taking its course in the reprobate … There is nothing inconsistent in this with the fact of his enlightening some with a present sense of grace, which afterward proves evanescent."[330] In other words, God can influence an unsaved man, through an "inferior operation of the Spirit," with a "present sense of grace" so that, in his own mind and judgment, he considers himself to be saved and elect of God, but once he falls away, he demonstrates that his faith was "evanescent" and that he was never saved in the first place. Calvin, of course, is correct that what he states is not inconsistent with his theological system, but it is inconsistent with the Scriptures, which limit the assurance of salvation to those who are actually saved (Romans 8:16; Galatians 4:6).

Although John Calvin might be more straightforward in his expressions about this issue, it does not appear that he is at odds with other Reformed theologians. For example, in his popular *Systematic Theology*, Wayne Grudem concurs with the proposition that "only those who persevere to the end have been truly born again."[331] Therefore, if a "Christian" does not persevere to the end, he wasn't truly saved to begin with. In order to defend this position, Grudem spends a good deal of time explaining why certain passages, apparently, do not teach that true believers can fall away, such as Hebrews 6. Theologians who deny that true Christians can depart from the faith and forfeit their salvation wrestle with Hebrews 6:4-6:

> For it is impossible for those who were once enlightened, and have tasted of the heavenly gift, and were made partakers of the Holy Ghost, and

---

[329] Calvin, *Institutes of the Christian Religion*, 362. Emphasis mine.

[330] Ibid.

[331] Grudem, *Systematic Theology*, 792.

have tasted the good word of God, and the powers
of the world to come, if they shall fall away, to renew
them again unto repentance; seeing they crucify to
themselves the Son of God afresh, and put him to
an open shame.

There are several characteristics mentioned about these men
who have fallen away from the faith. Many Christians fail to see how
these descriptions could apply to an unregenerate person. But, due
to the requirements of his theology, Grudem explains what kind of
people he thinks Hebrews 6 is referring to. He writes:

> These are no doubt people who have been affiliated
> closely with the fellowship of the church. They have
> some sorrow for sin (repentance). They have clearly
> understood the gospel (they have been enlightened).
> They have come to appreciate the attractiveness of
> the Christian life and the change that comes about
> in people's lives because of becoming a Christian,
> and they have probably had answers to prayer in
> their own lives and felt the power of the Holy Spirit
> at work, perhaps even using some spiritual gifts ...
> They have thought about the gospel for years and
> have continued to resist the wooing of the Holy Spirit
> in their lives, perhaps through an unwillingness to
> give up lordship of their lives to Jesus and preferring
> to cling to it themselves.[332]

So, according to Grudem, these people gave many external signs
that they had been born of God, but the most important point for our

---

[332] Ibid., 799-800. This last statement is more than a little confusing.
How it is consistent for Grudem to maintain both irresistible grace and
the resistance of the Holy Spirit's wooing in some lives is beyond my finite
comprehension. Perhaps God has not ordained for me to grasp such a
convoluted idea.

current discussion is this: *Did they think that they had been born of God?* In feeling the Spirit of God at work in their lives, and in being used by God in spiritual gifts, did they, in their best judgment, consider themselves to be saved? These are not questions about whether they fooled everyone else. These are questions about whether they fooled themselves. To this, Grudem admits, "In Hebrews 6:4-5 these people's experience of the Holy Spirit's power and of the Word of God was of course a *genuine* experience (just as Jesus *genuinely* died), but that by itself does not show that the people had an experience of regeneration."[333] That is to say, to a Calvinist, people can have as authentic an experience as Christ's death, to such a degree that *they consider themselves to be regenerated*, yet not actually be regenerated.

To summarize, both John Calvin and Wayne Grudem, along with other Calvinist theologians, maintain that some people are influenced by God in a way that they consider themselves to be saved, even though they are not saved and will ultimately be damned for eternity. If that is the case, can a believer really know that he is saved? I answer with a resounding *no*.

In his magnificent work *Life in the Son*, Robert Shank powerfully addresses this same issue that Calvinism creates. He asks:

> How can it be known whether one's calling and justification are actual, or only imagined? How can it be known whether one's experience of God's grace is divinely intended to be permanent, or only temporary? How can it be known whether God has implanted within him 'the living root of faith' which is ordained to endure, or whether his faith eventually must prove to have been only 'evanescent?'"[334]

Obviously, the only way it can be known is through perseverance. But how long must a person persevere until he knows that he is actually saved? As Wayne Grudem confessed, "Those

---

[333] Ibid., 797-798. Italics his.
[334] Shank, *Life in the Son*, 293.

whose faith is not real will *eventually* fall away from participation in the fellowship of the church."³³⁵ Notice the italicized word in the previous statement. *Eventually* is not a scientific measurement; it is very ambiguous. *Eventually* could mean one week, one month, one year, or one decade. Logically, then, according to the implications of Calvinism, a person could persevere for many years, hold positions in the church, lead souls to Christ, experience answers to prayer, and consider himself to be saved, yet fall away from the faith and demonstrate that he had deceived both himself and others in spite of the evidence to the contrary.

My argument has been that Calvinism removes the possibility for a Christian having assurance of his salvation. Because of how Calvinists describe saving faith as necessarily enduring to the end and God affecting those not truly saved in a manner that they consider themselves to be saved, no Calvinist can have genuine assurance until his death. He might be a reprobate that God has "affected in a way so similar to the elect, that even *in [his] own judgment* there is no difference between them."³³⁶ This theological position seems fraught with practical problems that would cause serious anxiety for any of its adherents.

Fortunately, the Bible doesn't teach Calvinism. Christians can have assurance that they are in Christ and have been adopted into his family. They don't have to doubt whether the signs of assurance aren't valid. Whoever believes in the Lord Jesus Christ (John 3:16), is walking in obedience to his commands (John 14:15), loves the people of God (1 John 3:14), and is bearing the fruit of the Spirit (Galatians 5:22,23) has eternal life. Only Christians can possess the assurance of salvation. There is not need to worry if, perhaps, God, by "an inferior operation of the Spirit" has enlightened you "with a present sense of grace" so that, in your own judgment, you think that you are saved even though you are not. If the Spirit testifies to you that you belong to Christ, then you need to rejoice in this blessed assurance, not fret over whether God is toying with you by giving you a false sense of assurance.

---

³³⁵ Grudem, *Systematic Theology*, 793. Italics mine.
³³⁶ Calvin, *Institutes of the Christian Religion*, 362.

Can a Christian Lose His Salvation?

Closely related to the topic of a Christian's assurance is the idea of persevering faith. We have mentioned this briefly, but it is an integral part to the entire discussion. Can a true believer forfeit his salvation? Or do the Scriptures teach that once a person experiences the saving grace of Jesus Christ, he will always be saved? Generations of sincere, godly men have stood on both sides of the debate, arguing for their particular interpretation of the Scriptures.

Again, what must be the final authority for this discussion is the word of God. The Bible- not your parents, or your tradition, or even your pastor- should be the ultimate authority for deciding doctrinal questions. Many men have begun their study of the Scriptures with presuppositions that necessitate their conclusions. They start with their mind settled on what the Bible teaches about a specific issue. In other words, their theology precedes and governs their exegesis. This is a reverse of the proper order. Our theology must be derived from the Scriptures. We should believe what we believe, not because that is what we want to believe, but because that is what the Bible teaches.

Some have framed this debate as if there are equal number of verses on either side. For instance, theologian Lewis Sperry Chafer wrote, "While the great body of New Testament Scriptures which bear directly or indirectly on this question declare the believer to be secure, there are upwards of twenty-five passages which have been cited in evidence by those who maintain that the believer is insecure."[337] What he means by this, of course, is that although, in his view, the "great body of New Testament Scriptures" teach unconditional eternal security, some passages seem to contradict this position. Therefore, since the majority is right, those troublesome texts must be conformed to agree with the rest of the Bible that seemingly supports the inevitable perseverance of believers.

Chafer commits the same mistake many others unfortunately make by insisting that those who maintain that a true believer can

---

[337] Lewis Sperry Chafer, *Major Bible Themes* (Wheaton, IL: Van Kampen Press, 1953), 187.

apostatize do not think that the believer is secure. This is simply false. Robert Shank argues this well, "Many who have debated 'the security of the believer' have missed the issue. The question is not, Is the believer secure? but rather, What is a believer?"[338] The Bible is abundantly clear that the believer is secure. No Christian should disagree with this assertion. However, the believer is secure *only* as long as he continues to be a believer. Christians will be presented "holy and unblameable and unreproveable" in God's sight, provided that they "continue in the faith grounded and settled, and be not moved away from the hope of the gospel" (Colossians 1:21-23). Only those who endure to the end will be finally saved (Matthew 24:13; John 8:51). Any believer who fails to abide in Christ will be cut off from his relationship with the Savior because of a failure to "continue in [God's] goodness" (Romans 11:17-23).

This thesis of the security of the believer conditioned on his continuing faith can be seen throughout the New Testament. Consider, for example, John 10:27-29. John writes a blessed promise:

> My sheep hear my voice, and I know them, and they follow me: and I give unto them eternal life; and they shall never perish, neither shall any man pluck them out of my hand. My Father, which gave them me, is greater than all; and no man is able to pluck them out of my Father hand.

This passage contains a precious guarantee: a follower of Christ cannot be plucked out of God's hand by any external force or enemy. It is similar to Paul's confidence in Romans 8:38,39 that nothing would be "able us to separate from the love of God, which is in Christ our Lord." As long as a believer remains in Christ, he has the assurance that nothing could sever his relationship with Jesus. Frederick Louis Godet asked this question about the promises of John 10: "Can this guarantee insure believers against the consequences

---

[338] Shank, *Life in the Son*, 55.

of their own unfaithfulness?"[339] Advocates of unconditional eternal security respond in the affirmative. This conclusion is erroneous. Godet's answer to his own question is correct: "The question is of enemies from without who seek to carry off the sheep, but not of unfaithfulness through which the sheep would themselves cease to be sheep."[340] Eminent biblical scholar Ben Witherington III concurs, "Both John 10:28 and Romans 8:28-39 are texts meant to reassure that no outside force or being can snatch one out of the firm grasp of God. They do not address the issue of apostasy."[341]

A close examination of John 10:27-29 supports Godet's interpretation. The splendid promise of God's protective power is mentioned after the "specific condition governing our Saviour's promise."[342] Jesus declared, "My sheep hear my voice, and I know them, and they follow me, and I give unto them eternal life ..." All four of these verbs (hear, know, follow, give) are present indicatives. These indicate continuous action, not a punctiliar event. It's not a one-time hearing, knowing, following, and giving; it's a continual hearing, knowing, following, and giving. Dale Moody offered an expanded translation to help communicate the ongoing nature of these verbs: "My sheep keep on hearing my voice, and I keep on knowing them, and they keep on following me: and I keep on giving them eternal life ..."[343] Thus, the guarantee of John 10 applies only to those who meet the condition of listening to the voice of Jesus and following him.

Someone might object to this by saying, "But John 10 says that Jesus gives eternal life. If eternal life can be lost, then it isn't eternal." This popular objection could be brought from any number of passages that assign eternal life to the person who believes (John 3:16; 3:36; 5:24). This argument arises, however, from two understandable

[339] Frederick L. Godet, *Commentary on the Gospel of John- Vol. II* (Grand Rapids, Mi: Zondervan), 162.
[340] Ibid.
[341] Witherington III, *John's Wisdom*, 389.
[342] Shank, *Life in the Son*, 56.
[343] Moody, *The Word of Truth*, 356-357.

misunderstandings. First, it assumes that eternal is being used as an adverb, not an adjective. In the phrase "eternal life," eternal describes life, not a person's possession of it.[344] A Christian has eternal life; he does not necessarily have eternal life *eternally*. Eternal life is only found in a personal relationship with Jesus Christ.

In the Scriptures, this relationship with Jesus Christ is seen as an ongoing, day-by-day reality. Robert Shank articulates this well, "Throughout his earthly sojourn, the relation of the individual to Christ is never a *static* relationship existing as the irrevocable consequence of a past decision, act, or experience. Rather, it is a present mutual indwelling of the believer and the Saviour, the sharing of a common life which emanates from Him 'who is our life' (Colossians 3:4)."[345] Eternal life is only available in union with Jesus Christ. As long as a Christian abides in him, he has eternal life, but if he departs from Christ, he forfeits eternal life.

This leads us to the second misunderstanding. We must ask ourselves, "What exactly is eternal life?" Some might automatically assume that it refers to "endless existence."[346] But this would seem to be unnecessary, given that God created human beings with immortality. From the beginning of time, endless existence has been the possession of every person in the world. Everybody will live eternally either in heaven or in hell. Eternal life, then, does not merely refer to endless existence. Rather, as A. T. Robertson said, "It is more than endless [life], for it is sharing in the life of God in Christ."[347] Eternal life is a particular quality of life found in a restored relationship with God through the Lord Jesus Christ.

The idea that a person is "once saved, always saved," regardless of any eventualities in his life, is foreign to the testimony of the

---

[344] Ibid., 356. Moody stated, "They work with the false assumption that the adjective "eternal" is an adverb, as if it says the brother eternally has life. It is the life that is eternal, not one's possession of it. Eternal life is the life of God in Christ the Son of God."

[345] Shank, *Life in the Son*, 42-43.

[346] Ibid., 21.

[347] Robertson, *Word Pictures in the New Testament- Vol. IV*, 50.

Bible. A true believer can forfeit his salvation by departing from the true and living God (Hebrews 3:12). Proof of this position can be found in the abundance of passages that warn believers to continue in the faith. For instance, Jesus admonished his disciples, "Take heed that no man deceive you ... Many false prophets shall rise, and shall deceive many ... But he that shall endure to the end, the same shall be saved" (Matthew 24:4,11,13). In predicting that "many false prophets" will "deceive many," Jesus warned his disciples to be careful so that "no man deceive *you*." Only those who faithfully endure until the end will be finally saved. Any follower of Christ, including one of Jesus' first disciples, who is deceived by a false prophet will not be saved in the end because his love for God has grown cold (v. 12).

It must be asked: Why would Jesus warn his disciples about these false teachers if it was impossible for them to lose their salvation? Since the disciples were undoubtedly saved, the warning of Jesus would be hypothetical at best if it was literally impossible from them to be deceived by false prophets. The reason why Jesus warned his disciples about the false teachers is because it was exceedingly perilous to listen to and accept their message. That his disciples would persevere in faith to the end was not an ironclad guarantee but demanded their wholehearted commitment to remain faithful to the teachings of Christ in the midst of false prophets.

Paul's methodology in the book of Acts is consistent with Jesus' exhortation to endure to the end. Luke, the author of Acts, writes, "And when they [Paul and Barnabas] had preached the gospel to that city, and had taught many, they returned again to Lystra, and to Iconium, and Antioch, confirming the souls of the disciples, and *exhorting them to continue in the faith*, and that we must through much tribulation enter into the kingdom of God" (Acts 14:20,21). Quite clearly, Paul encouraged these young converts to continue in the faith precisely because it was possible for them to not continue in the faith. In order to enter the kingdom of God, it was necessary for them to endure tribulation and "cleave unto the Lord" (Acts 11:23).

Sadly, not every person who becomes a Christian remains a Christian. This is confirmed in Luke's account of the parable of the Sower (Luke 8:1-18). Here, there is a group of people who when they hear the gospel preached "receive" it with joy, but have no root, so "for a while believe, and in time of temptation fall away" (v. 13). The key question to be asked is whether this believing was unto salvation. There is no doubt that the Greek word for *believe* is used in the New Testament in instances that do not refer to saving faith, such as its use in connection with "the devils" in James 2:19. However, context must determine the meaning of *believe* in Luke 8:13. Robert Shank highlights the context, "The use of the word [believe] in verse 12 establishes its meaning as it is employed in the parable. It is clearly a believing unto salvation: '. ... lest they should believe and be saved.'"[348] To assign a different interpretation to the believing in verse 13 than is expressed in verse 12 is to reveal one's theological bias. Those described in verse 13 were truly saved as long as they believed, but deserted this privileged position when they fell away during a time of testing.

Not only are there stern warnings in the New Testament against the danger of departing from Christ, but there are also examples of men who committed apostasy and walked away from Christ. Paul described two in 1 Timothy 1:19,20. He writes about some that have shipwrecked their faith, "of whom is Hymenaeus and Alexander." John Wesley used this passage to disprove the doctrine of the inevitable perseverance of the saints. His argument was simple: Hymenaeus and Alexander, along with the other apostates, "had once the faith that purifies the heart, that produces a good conscience; which they once had, or they could not have 'put it away.'"[349] This seems like common sense, but, unfortunately, sometimes, certain men's theology allows no place for common sense. If these men had not possessed the faith, they could not have shipwrecked it. You cannot shipwreck a boat that you were not sailing on.

---

[348] Shank, *Life in the Son*, 32.
[349] Wesley, *The Works of John Wesley- Vol. X*, 283.

A final passage that reveals the possibility of apostasy for true believers occurs in 2 Peter. Peter describes the situation of these apostate, false teachers:

> For if after they have escaped the pollutions of the world through the knowledge of the Lord and Saviour Jesus Christ, they are again entangled therein, and overcome, the latter end is worse with them than the beginning. For it had been better for them not to have known the way of righteousness, than, after they have known it, to turn from the holy commandment delivered unto them. But it is happened unto them according to the true proverb, 'The dog is turned to his own vomit again; and the sow that was washed to her wallowing in the mire'" (2 Peter 2:20-22).

These apostates had been delivered through the "knowledge of the Lord and Saviour Jesus Christ." This was not just a mere intellectual knowledge of the facts, but "a way of representing the saving knowledge of Christ one gains at conversion."[350] They had been delivered from their former sinful lifestyles by embracing the "way of truth" (v. 2). However, they had turned from the "holy commandment" that had been delivered to them and, consequently, had been entangled again by the pollutions of the world. According to Peter, their current state is worse than it would have been had they never known "the way of righteousness." His illustrations provide vivid descriptions of this sad tragedy. Robert Picirilli's comment is fitting, "Like a dog that comes back to lick up the spoiled vomit that sickened him in the first place, like a sow that gets a bath and goes back to the mud from which she had been cleansed, these apostates return to the enslaving, polluting wickedness from which they had been delivered."[351] Peter holds up these apostate teachers in front of

---

[350] Picirilli, *Grace, Faith, Free Will*, 230.
[351] Ibid., 232.

his audience to show them the devastation that awaits them if they return to the corruption of the world.

The New Testament evidence leads to the conclusion that a Christian can depart from the faith and forfeit his salvation. He does this consciously, not accidentally. As Ben Witherington III puts it so plainly, "A believer cannot lose his salvation, like one might lose one's glasses. But by willful rebellion there is the possibility of apostasy, of making shipwreck of one's faith. The good news, then, is that one cannot lose or misplace one's salvation or simply wander away by accident. Indeed, only by an enormous willful effort could one throw it away."[352] As Christians, we should rejoice that we are secure in our salvation. We are being "kept by the power of God … unto salvation ready to be revealed in the last time" (1 Peter 1:5). However, it is *through faith* that we are secure. God's keeping power does not avail for men who are not willing to be kept. It is our duty to *keep* ourselves in the love of God by building up ourselves in the faith, praying in the Holy Ghost, and looking forward to the return of Christ (Jude 20, 21). Certainly, if we abide in Christ by faithfully keeping his commandments (John 15:10), he will abide in us, and nothing can pluck us out of the Father's hand (John 10:29).

---

[352] Ben Witherington III, *The Problem with Evangelical Theology* (Waco, TX: Baylor University Press, 2005), 83.

CHAPTER 9

The Danger of Calvinism

There are many dangers of Calvinism for Christians to be aware of. Throughout this book, we have attempted to expose the practical, biblical, and theological errors of Reformed theology. Along the way, hopefully, you have begun to see how dangerous Calvinism is. In this chapter, several distinct dangers of Calvinism will be examined. Some of these are explicitly taught by Calvinists, while other dangers are logical inferences. Nevertheless, it is important to understand these dangers in order to avoid succumbing to this false doctrine.

The Danger of Antinomianism

Antinomianism is "the false teaching that since faith alone is necessary for salvation, one is free from the moral obligation of the law ... While it is true that obedience to the law will never earn salvation for anyone (Ephesians 2:8-9), it is equally true that those who are saved are expected to live a life full of good works (Ephesians

2:10)."[353] It is clear that grace does not cancel the moral law, and this kind of heresy is exposed in Paul's writings (1 Corinthians 5-6 and Romans 6: 1-2). Historic Christianity has rejected the view that grace gives a moral license to the believer and, in fact, teaches the opposite. This truth is profoundly emphasized in Galatians 5:24: "They that are Christ's have crucified the flesh with the affections and lusts."

One of the most disparaging doctrinal errors that Calvinism introduces is an omission of the necessity of sanctification by moving directly from justification to the perseverance of the saints, which leads, practically, to antinomianism. The Christian community "argued that antinomians misunderstood the nature of justification by faith, which, though granted apart from the works of the law, is not sanctification."[354] It is true that we are justified by faith, but the faith that justifies is not alone. As theologian Millard Erickson observed, "The genuineness of the faith that leads to justification becomes apparent in the results that issue from it. If there are no good works, there has been neither real faith nor justification."[355]

The fallacious belief that justification seals the believer eternally, regardless of his behavior after his conversion, is a travesty. One may claim the occurrence of any event, but the evidentiary aspect of that event is required. For example, Jesus presented Himself alive after His resurrection by many infallible proofs (Acts 1:3). Likewise, the Scriptures note the evidence of salvation by revealing that those born of God will manifest love for the brethren (1 John 3:14) and have a new identity in Christ (2 Corinthians 5:17). In addition, James clearly indicated there must be evidentiary manifestations in order for faith to be considered saving, for he wrote, "Ye see then how that by works a man is justified, and not by faith only" (James 2:24), and "For as the body without the spirit is dead, so faith without works is dead also" (James 2:26).

---

[353] Trent C. Butler, ed., *Holman Bible Dictionary* (Nashville, TN: Holman Bible Publishers, 1991), 64.

[354] Elwell, *Evangelical Dictionary of Theology*, 59.

[355] Erickson, *Christian Theology*, 890.

The assumption that the righteousness and holiness of Jesus Christ is imputed *only* is erroneous biblical interpretation. As Purkiser, Taylor, and Taylor write, "To assume that those who are in Christ participate in His sanctification in the sense that it is credited to them by virtue of this union without being accomplished in them, is to miss the redemptive genius of our Lord, who makes us like himself."[356] Again, the Bible clearly teaches that man is not saved by good works. However, the Bible also clearly teaches that works follow in a life that is regenerated by the power of God. The Christian understands it is not his righteousness but the righteousness of Jesus Christ that receives all glory and praise. It should be noted that the importance of good works is seen in that they reveal the Christian's love for God. They also manifest a desire to be a testimony and bring glory to God. Finally, good works reveal obedience to the Word of God and the Holy Spirit. Consequently, good works are necessary evidentiary aspects of regeneration and faith toward God.

The false teaching of antinomianism deceives many. Since the Calvinists advocate that in justification one is sealed eternally, they argue that sanctification does not affect a believer's eternal destiny. There are many who surrendered the passion for a sanctified. Since that struggle ended, there is a false belief that they understand grace in a greater depth and are closer to God than ever before when, in reality, they are backsliding. Professor H. C. Thiessen offered a warning: "The Scriptures so far from condoning sin in the life of the believer, definitely prohibit it and demand that we live an overcoming life ... The Apostle warns the Corinthians that those who live in sin 'shall not inherit the kingdom of God' (1 Corinthians 6:10)."[357]

Sanctification is the will of God according to 1 Thessalonians 4:3. Apostle Paul continued with this thought in 1 Thessalonians 5:23 when he admonished the saints to be sanctified in body, soul, and spirit. A careful and extensive study of Scripture reveals two important truths about sanctification. First, one is sanctified by

---

[356] Purkiser, Taylor, and Taylor, *God, Man, & Salvation*, 467.

[357] Thiessen, *Introductory Lectures In Systematic Theology*, 383.

the blood of Christ, the Word of God, and the working of the Holy Ghost. Second, sanctification is positional, instantaneous, progressive, and practical. Tragically, Calvinism focuses only on positional standing and neglects and denigrates the relationship of progressive and practical sanctification in the life of the believer. Theologian Ralph Knudson noted, "Unless there is growth there is retrogression, even dismemberment of the fellowship. It is absurd to assume that an initial experience with Christ is all that one needs for the continuation of the Christian life."[358]

Calvinism proclaims that when we were saved, "we were made perfectly, totally, and forever holy in God's sight regardless of what we do or how we live."[359] This erroneous interpretation of Scripture has deceived multitudes into believing that they are saved and that no matter how they live they are eternally secure. However, the Christian life calls for progression in the understanding of the defilement of sin. 2 Corinthians 6: 14-19 commands and commends the sanctified life and the deepening relationship between God the Father and the child of God. 2 Corinthians 7:1 challenges the Christian to live a life of separation perfecting holiness in the fear of God. Progressive and practical sanctification reveal movement toward God, a rich growing relationship with God, and is the anecdote for apostasy.

The tragedy of Reformed Theology is apparent in the following quotation of two well-known Calvinists: "True believers do fall into temptations, and they do commit grievous sins, but *these sins do not cause them to lose their salvation or separate them from Christ.*"[360] This causes many to accept that lasciviousness, concupiscence, social drinking, deviate behavior, and other grievous sins are not disqualifiers from the kingdom of God. However, Calvinists are quick to respond that in the end those who manifest such actions were never in grace in

---

[358] Ralph E. Knudsen, *Theology in the New Testament* (Chicago, IL: The Judson Press, 1964), 298.

[359] Michael L. Brown, *Hyper-Grace* (Lake Mary, FL: Charisma House, 2014), 92.

[360] Steele and Thomas, *The Five Points of Calvinism*, 56. Italics mine.

the first place. Clearly, to maintain such a convoluted perspective eliminates the possibility of any Christian having the assurance of his salvation. Shank's conclusion is right: "It is obviously an error of the gravest sort to assume that a past experience of conversion makes one unconditionally secure and constitutes a guarantee of final salvation."[361]

One can readily see the lukewarm, ungodly behavioral patterns of lifestyle potentially produced by believing in Calvinism. For example, the Scriptures teach that I should not sin. However, when I sin, it apparently has been predetermined by God that I should sin, even though he wrote in his word that I shouldn't sin. Thus, when I do sin, and if I believed in Calvinism, it would be easy to justify my sinning. After all, God had determined that I should sin in exactly the way that I did sin. Indeed, as McCall notes, "Surely any metaphysical system that produces these results is one that is ill-suited for a biblically and theologically adequate doctrine of sanctification ... these contradictions at the heart of a theological system produce imbalances in the Christian life."[362]

Theologians David Allen and Steve Lemke revealed in their book *Whosoever Will* profitable insight into the Calvinistic approach to ecclesiology. They write, "The first thing to note about Calvinist ecclesiology is that, in spite of its methodological claim for sola scriptura, Calvinism typically moves beyond the Bible in order to create its theological standards."[363] An example of such theological maneuvering is that of John Calvin, who "introduced the doctrine of 'forbearance' as a foil to the doctrine of the regenerate church."[364] He promoted the idea of accepting fellowship with the unregenerate, evil sinner. While he recognized that "the wicked should ideally not be present in the church, one must still not separate them."[365] Allen and Lemke contend, "Although he saw church discipline as

---

[361] Shank, *Life in the Son*, 298.

[362] McCall, "We Believe in God's Sovereign Goodness," 244.

[363] Allen and Lemke, *Whosoever Will*, 215.

[364] Ibid., 229.

[365] Ibid., 229.

the sinews of the church, he did not consider it necessary for the church."[366]

To justify his erroneous interpretation of biblical truth concerning ecclesiology, Calvin posited the idea of necessary doctrine and nonessential matters. Allen and Lemke noted, "The separation of essential from nonessential doctrines has been part and parcel of Calvinism's ecclesiological antinomianism. Often theological doctrines are defined as essential while ethical and ecclesiological doctrines are defined as nonessential."[367] This type of theological gymnastics and innovations leads to aristocratic elitism. This is effectively revealed with "the aristocratic tendency and the related Calvinist use of synods and assemblies above the church."[368] Such tendencies clearly contradict the New Testament teaching concerning the autonomy of the local New Testament church.

In conclusion, Professor Wilbur Tillett, in his book *Personal Salvation,* effectively and emphatically noted the horrendous danger of antinomianism. He stressed the point that the rejection of moral law, the denial of the necessity of good works and a life of sanctification, and the erroneous doctrine of divine determinism leads to the belief "that all regenerate believers not only do sin in word, thought, and deed, but many sin grievously and scandalously without forfeiting their title to the skies -- is a doctrine the preaching of which is fraught with untold peril, and it is calculated to lead men into sin rather than make them void sin."[369]

The Danger of the Negated Role of the Holy Spirit

The first major point to address is the salvific ministry of the Holy Spirit in evangelism. The Calvinist rejects the idea of the gospel

---

[366] Ibid., 228.

[367] Ibid., 230.

[368] Ibid., 227.

[369] Wilbur Tillett, *Personal Salvation* (Nashville: Publishing House of the M.E. Church, South, 1902), 369.

invitation to salvation, insisting that because of total inability man cannot choose spiritual good. Therefore, God has unconditionally elected whom He chooses to be saved and will regenerate them with man contributing nothing. The idea of man making a decision to accept Jesus as one's Lord and Savior is foreign to the Calvinist. However, in John 16:8, the Bible, in reference to evangelism and the Holy Ghost, states, "And when he is come, he will reprove the world of sin, and of righteousness, and of judgment." The first work of the Holy Ghost is convicting the unbeliever of his sinful state. When this occurs there is the call and opportunity of repentance by exercising one's free will while under conviction of the Holy Ghost. Apostle Paul established this truth when he wrote in 2 Corinthians 7:10, " For godly sorrow worketh repentance to salvation not to be repented of; but the sorrow of the world worketh death."

Jesus presented the gospel invitation in Matthew 11:28-30 when He declared, "Come unto me, all ye that labour and are heavy laden, and I will give you rest. Take my yoke upon you, and learn of me; for I am meek and lowly in heart: and ye shall find rest unto your souls. For my yoke is easy, and my burden is light." Albert Barnes noted that, in this passage, "there can be no doubt that He meant here chiefly to address the poor, lost, ruined sinner ... Christ tells them to come to Him, to believe in Him, and to trust Him, and Him only for salvation. Doing this, he will give them rest--rest from their sins, from the alarms of conscience, from the terrors of the law, and from the fears of eternal death."[370]

There are many other scriptural references that justify the gospel invitation or altar call for salvation. The hermeneutical approach the Calvinist takes to respond to such powerful calls of God is to create terminology which is biblically unsound. In this case they make a distinction between a general outward call and a special inward call. According to Steele and Thomas, the general outward call "promises salvation to all who repent and believe. But this outward general call, extended to elect and non-elect alike, will not bring

---

[370] Albert Barnes, *Notes On The New Testament--Matthew and Mark* (Grand Rapids, MI: Baker Book House, 1980), 124.

sinners to Christ."[371] How tragic is such a false presentation! Why would the gospel be offered to sinners who have no opportunity for salvation? Why would the Holy Spirit convict people whom God has not elected for salvation? It seems that God would just be toying with such people, giving them an indication that they can be saved when God has rendered it certain that will not be saved.

Consider also the Calvinistic explanation of the special inward call of the gospel given to the elect. Steele and Thomas describe this peculiar doctrine: "This special call is not made to all sinners but is issued to the elect only. The Spirit is in no way dependent upon their help or cooperation for success in His work of bringing them to Christ."[372] They continue, "The Spirit creates within the sinner a new heart or a new nature ... His will is renewed through this process so that the sinner spontaneously comes to Christ of his own free choice."[373] Several egregious doctrinal biblical errors can be seen in respect to this special inward call. First, the Holy Spirit, according to Reformed theology, is restrictive in His reproving and extending of the blessing of salvation. However, John 3:16-17; John 16:8; I Timothy 2:4; and 2 Peter 3:9 all indicate salvation is for the whole world, not the limited world of the elect. Second, this special inward call fails to take seriously the repeated affirmations in Scripture of the Holy Spirit being rejected. As Stephen told those who were murdering him: "Ye stiffnecked and uncircumcised in heart and ears, ye do always resist the Holy Spirit" (Acts 7:51). Thomas Oden observed, "Stephen assumed that his persecutors were capable of resisting God, who had not compelled the will irresistibly."[374] Furthermore, the longsuffering of God toward those he loves would be a farce if he had determined for them to reject him and not receive his grace. To create theological innovations, such as the general outward call and the special inward call, and to invent radical interpretations that

---

[371] Steele and Thomas, *The Five Points of Calvinism*, 48.

[372] Ibid., 49.

[373] Ibid., 48.

[374] Thomas Oden, *The Transforming Power of Grace* (Nashville: Abingdon Press, 1993), 114.

conflict God's attributes, necessarily offends, violates, and distorts the scriptural revelation about God and his saving ways.

The second major point to address is the work of the Holy Spirit in sanctification. While sanctification was addressed earlier under antinomianism, it is vital to return to this topic and point out the work of the Holy Spirit in this very important doctrine. The continual work of the Holy Ghost in the sanctified life is emphatically established in Scripture. First Corinthians 6:11 and 2 Thessalonians 2:13 emphasize the work of the Holy Spirit. Romans 15:16b states, 'being sanctified by the Holy Ghost." 1 Peter 1:2 states, 'through sanctification of the Spirit." In addition, the fulfillment of the fruit of the Spirit is accomplished by the work of the Spirit of God according to Galatians 5: 22-23. Finally, Paul reminds us, "If we live in the Spirit, let us also walk in the Spirit" (Galatians 5:25).

A life of dedication and separation is required biblically, and is commended and sanctioned by the Holy Ghost. Associations, allegiances, activities, appearances, and agendas, just to name a few, are to be controlled by the Word of God and the work of the Holy Ghost. This allows the Christian life to present and portray a righteous, holy God. All of the aforementioned areas do matter in the Christian life. Carnal, worldly appetites clearly indicate a Christian has not set his affections on things above, but on things of this earth (Colossians 3:1). This is not legalism but liberty! This is not man's determination, but God's directive. This is not an attitude of self-works, but an attitude of submissive worship.

The failure of Calvinism to recognize the necessity of sanctification leads to the dangerous situation that every man can do that which is right in his own eyes and it will not affect his eternal destiny. Godet, in his commentary on Romans, noted, "For the guidance of the Spirit tends constantly to the sacrifice of the flesh; and if the believer refuses to follow it on his path, he renounces the life of the Spirit and its glorious privileges."[375] Distinguished theologian Myer Pearlman summarized this point precisely when he wrote, "The operation of the Spirit is progressive, going from the

---

[375] Qtd in Shank, *Life in the Son*, 198.

heart to the surface, from the interior to the exterior, from the seat of life, to the manifestation of life, to the actions and to the words … nothing being able to escape His influence, one day the entire man, glorified by the Spirit, will be resplendent with the life of God."[376]

The third major point to address is the work of the Holy Ghost in spiritual gifts. Most Calvinists hold to the doctrine of cessationism, which rejects the manifestations of the gifts of the Holy Spirit such as healing, prophecy, and speaking in tongues. An erroneous interpretation of the phrase "whether there be tongues, they shall cease" in 1 Corinthians 13:8 has lead to a false conclusion of 1 Corinthians 13:8-12 and consequently the fallacious doctrine of cessationism. Cessationists generally argue that tongues ceased with the completion of the Bible. They assert that spiritual gifts were signs that ended with the apostolic era. However, the consideration of 1 Corinthians 13:8-12 in its entirety yields the realization that "there is not the slightest inference in the New Testament that any endowment of the Holy Spirit would cease before seeing 'face to face."[377] In addition, one historical survey of the early church, conducted by Ronald Kydd, demonstrated that "the gifts of the Spirit continued into the third century."[378] There is no indication that the gifts "were removed from the church by the Holy Spirit"[379] but that the secularization of the Church affected the desire for the manifestation of spiritual gifts. Also, writings of the early church fathers reveal their belief in the exercise of spiritual gifts. As Stanley Horton observed, "Justin Martyr defends the gifts of healings in the church of his day from the criticisms of a certain Trypho."[380] Augustine, after years of pastoring, acknowledged many miracles of

---

[376] Myer Pearlman, *Knowing the Doctrines of the Bible* (Springfield, MO: Gospel Publishing House, 1937), 308.

[377] Guy P. Duffield and Nathaniel M. Van Cleave, *Foundations of Pentecostal Theology* (Los Angeles, CA: Foursquare Media, 1987), 331.

[378] Stanley M. Horton, ed., *Systematic Theology* (Springfield, MO: Logion Press, 2003), 513.

[379] Ibid.

[380] Ibid.

healing in his pastorate.[381] A careful study of church history reveals that manifestations of spiritual gifts have occurred throughout the New Testament church age.

An unbiased exegesis of 1 Corinthians 13:8-12 will reveal that spiritual gifts, like tongues and prophecies, will continue throughout the church age until the coming of the Lord Jesus Christ. Albert Barnes observed about the gift of prophecy: "There shall be no further use for this gift in the light and glory of the world above, and it shall cease. God shall be the teacher there. And as there will be no need of conforming the truth of religion by the prediction of future events, and no need of warning against impending dangers there, the gift of foretelling future events will be of course unknown."[382] Concerning when tongues would cease, Barnes wrote, "The more natural interpretation is, to refer it to the future life; since the main idea which Paul is urging here is the value of love above all other endowments, from the fact that it would be abiding, or permanent."[383] While many more factors could be introduced, enough has been presented to come to a sound conclusion. The phrases "when that which is perfect is come," "we see through a glass, darkly; but then face to face," "then shall I know even as also I am known," are not talking about the canon of Scripture but the coming of Jesus Christ (the Perfect One) and Heaven (the place of full revelation and glory).

Cessationists often pointedly attack tongues and interpretation. These gifts are met with disdain and mockery and considered to be of minor and diminished value, inferior, and therefore listed last in 1 Corinthians 12:8-12. Nothing could be further from the truth. It should be noted that seven of the nine spiritual gifts listed in 1 Corinthians 12:8-12 occurred in the Old Testament. It is only logical that the two new manifestations of the Holy Ghost would be listed last. Also, chronological order does not necessarily establish priority. Is the last child born into a family any less important than

---

[381] Ibid., 514.

[382] Albert Barnes, *Notes on the New Testament - 1 Corinthians* (Grand Rapids, MI: Baker Book House, 1980), 253.

[383] Ibid., 253.

the firstborn? Is the Book of Revelation less inspired because it is the last book of the Bible? Is the twenty-first century church any less than the first-century church? The obvious answer to all these questions is absolutely not.

To suggest that the spiritual manifestation of gifts takes away, confuses, or overshadows the word of God is preposterous, since it is the Bible that teaches the existence of these spiritual gifts. Apostle Paul provides an excellent example to support this statement. To the Corinthians, who were influenced by the philosophical arguments of Socrates, Plato, and Aristotle, Paul wrote, "And my speech and my preaching was not with enticing words of man's wisdom, but in demonstration of the Spirit and power: that your faith should not stand in the wisdom of men, but in the power of God" (1 Corinthians 2:4-5). The author of the word of God is the authorizer and authority of the working of spiritual gifts. To attach the spiritual manifestations of the Holy Ghost to an aberrant or false gospel is blasphemous. Spiritual gifts are the manifestation of the Holy Ghost, the third Person of the Trinity. To assert that the gifts have ceased is to declare that our sovereign God is restricted in His manifestations to the church today. Finally, to compare false prophets, who abuse these spiritual gifts, with those who believe in and follow the Pentecostal doctrine of spiritual gifts is disingenuous. True adherents of Pentecostalism are quick to expose and rebuke false prophets and false doctrines. There are false professors of truth in all walks of life and religious organizations and fellowships. While intellectual elitism may be offended by emotional outbursts and manifestations of prophecy, tongues, and interpretations, the working and demonstration of the Holy Ghost will be a part of God's plan until the coming of Jesus Christ for his church. The manifestations of spiritual gifts are not to provide psychological, mental, or emotional gibberish, or a catharsis upheaval leaving one with an euphoric feeling, as some suggest. It is to be used by God, as a willing vessel, in spiritual demonstrations to edify, exhort, and comfort the church and glorify Jesus Christ. The belief that the gifts should continue to operate today is biblically, theologically, and historically justifiable and needed in these last days. However, one of the most dangerous aspects of Calvinism is its tendency to diminish the importance of these spiritual manifestations in the church.

Other Dangers of Calvinism

Calvinism brings into conflict the attributes. If Scripture interprets Scripture, why the contradictions, confusion, and creation of mysteries, categories, innovations, and secondary causes? Why the necessity to create theological and philosophical lenses through which the exegesis of Scripture is accomplished? When mysteries, categories, and secondary causes fail, the typical Calvinistic response to a refusal to accept this theological doublespeak is: "You just don't understand." Several examples will be given to illustrate this point of intellectual elitism.

First, it is hard to understand any argument when the argument contains two contradictory statements that are alleged to both be true. For instance, Calvinists argue that in order for God to be considered sovereign, he has determined all things in the history of mankind. They also want to insist that humans are responsible for their actions. They insist that both divine determinism and human responsibility are true, but how can this be? To our minds, this is certainly a contradiction. In response to this obvious dilemma, Calvinists often punt to mystery or reply that we should just accept what the Bible teaches, not try to reconcile it. However, the only reason for this contradiction is because they have misinterpreted God's sovereignty.

Two further things should be noted. First, their definition of sovereignty is wrong because it makes God's sovereignty arbitrary, instead of absolute, which makes God whimsical and capricious. Second, human responsibility is fulfilled through libertarian free will, which is denied by the Calvinist. However, "with the exception of the later Augustine, this view of self-determined free will was the virtually unanimous view of the Fathers up to the time of the Reformation, and with the exception of Calvin and Luther, it has continued to be the consistent view since the time of the Reformation."[384] Therefore, God, in His sovereignty, created man with a free will, and his eternal destiny is dependent upon accepting or rejecting Jesus Christ as his Savior and Lord.

Second, it is hard to understand how God can withhold Christ's atonement from the non-elect and then condemn them to the Lake of Fire for all eternity for not accepting what was never offered to them. This Calvinistic teaching brings into conflict the sovereignty of God with His omni-benevolence, mercy, and justice. How can you explain to the non-elect that God's grace is more magnified because of their damnation? Is it possible to explain to the non-elect that God is impartial, equitable in character and act, and no respecter of persons even though he chose a good portion of humanity to be eternally damned? It is callously arrogant to say that God graciously allowed the non-elect to receive what they desired when in fact God predestinated them to have those desires. Clearly, "it certainly would be contradictory to divine justice to condemn people to eternal separation from God for not living according to a standard they never had and never knew."[385] The fallacious doctrine of unconditional election leads to hopelessness for the non-elect and a false hope of being eternally chosen and sealed no matter one's choices or lifestyle. To suggest and even advocate a doctrine whereby all men do not have an opportunity to know the only true God makes God out to be a moral monster and whimsical tyrant. However, the sovereign God of Scripture does not contradict His attributes, and according to the various passages in the Bible, such as John 3:16; 1 Timothy 2:4; 1 Timothy 4:10; and 2 Peter 3:9, his omni-benevolence, mercy, and justice work in harmony, extending salvation freely to all men.

Third, it is hard to understand why there are so many warnings about apostasy in the Bible if the doctrine of unconditional eternal security is true. It is dangerous to teach that once a person is saved,

---

[384] Geisler, *Systematic Theology in One Volume*, 755.
[385] Ibid., 1204.

he is always saved. To explain apostasy in the life of the believer, Calvinists create terminology to defend this erroneous doctrine. Phrases such as "you cannot fall from grace, so you never were in grace;" "one loses fellowship, not sonship;" and "the believer was just a professor, not a possessor of salvation" are employed. The Scriptures speak plainly and emphatically that true believers can lose their salvation. Verses in the Bible, such as 1 Timothy 3:5-6; 2 Peter 2:20-21; Ezekiel 18:24; John 15:1-10; and Hebrews 2:1-4; 3:7-4:13; 6:1-19; and 10:19-39, all give grave warnings of apostasy. In addition, Galatians 2:21 states, "I do not frustrate the grace of God." The word frustrate means to make void, disannul nullify, or set at naught. Clearly, Apostle Paul believed it was a possibility to make void the grace of God in a believer's life. Also, Galatians 5:4 states, "ye are fallen from the grace of God." The word fallen means to drop away, to lose, and to make of none effect. To attempt to try to apply these verses to fellowship, service, and rewards is not only hermeneutical dishonesty, but dangerous to the jeopardizing of the souls of men.

CONCLUSION

Unless you have been hiding under a rock for the past few years, you are probably aware of the resurgence of Calvinism. Men and women, but especially men, have become enraptured by the theology of French Reformer John Calvin, although they rarely learn about this theology from Calvin himself. Those who accept these controversial doctrines often become quite dogmatic and seek to convert everyone they know to this new revelation. Calvinists themselves recognize this reality, warn against it, and label anyone guilty of this as experiencing a phenomenon known as "cage-stage Calvinism." Nevertheless, in spite of Calvinists' warning against this obnoxious attitude, many of the young, restless, and Reformed[386] continue to disrupt local congregations with their persistence in championing this theological system and converting whosoever will believe the message.

Why has Calvinism undergone a resurgence? Well, if Calvinism were true, it would be a mystery, since the God who has determined all things has also determined for a majority of his children to not embrace Calvinism. This makes no sense, except to those who have accepted the theology of John Calvin. Assuming, then, that Calvinism is not true, we believe that Calvinism has resurged due to the tremendous job of its primary spokespersons in spreading this theology. John Piper, John MacArthur, R. C. Sproul, James White,

---

[386] This expression (young, restless, and Reformed) was coined by Collin Hansen to describe this new revival of Calvinism. He wrote a book by this title: Collin Hansen, *Young, Restless, Reformed* (Wheaton: Crossway, 2008).

Ligon Duncan, Al Mohler, Kevin DeYoung, and Mark Dever- to name a few- have filled the bookstores with their books and have saturated the airwaves with their sermons and lectures.

Jerry Walls, in his book *Does God Love Everyone?*, acknowledges that "Calvinists have done a better job getting their message out through both scholarly and popular books."[387] He tells the story of taking a trip to Brazil to teach theology at different Assemblies of God churches and colleges. During his trip, he "visited two large Christian bookstores in Brazil, and was struck by the number of books by noted Calvinist theologians and biblical scholars that had been translated into Portuguese."[388] This phenomenon even occurred at one of these Assemblies of God bookstores. Indeed, Wall's experience in Brazil is *not* limited in scope to Brazil. One of the primary reasons for the increase in popularity of Calvinism, both in America and around the world, is that Calvinists have done a great job of spreading their message.

Furthermore, Calvinism is an attractive alternative to the weak, water-downed theology offered by most American pastors and preachers. Walls and Dongell observe, "Part of Calvinism's attraction is surely that it represents a stark alternative to the superficial, seeker-sensitive theology that predominates in many churches in America."[389] Young Christians, desiring to get a deeper understanding of the Scriptures, are confronted with the alternative of Calvinism through a book by Sproul, a sermon by Piper, or a lecture by White, and are unprepared to respond to the arguments presented by these Calvinists since they have been fed a diet of sermons that more closely resembles an inspirational pep talk than genuine biblical exposition. When a young Christian encounters Calvinism for the first time and compares it to theology he has been taught for his entire life, thinking that these are the only two options available, he chooses Calvinism because it offers a more robust, thoughtful theology.

---

[387] Jerry Walls, *Does God Love Everyone?* (Eugene: Cascade Books, 2016), x.
[388] Ibid.
[389] Walls and Dongell, *Why I Am Not a Calvinist*, 17.

How should we respond, then, to this resurgence of Reformed theology? First, we should provide careful *biblical* answers. Generally, but not always, Calvinists become Calvinists because they honestly think that this is what the Bible teaches. Of course, we don't think that the Bible teaches Calvinism, but simply asserting that the Bible doesn't teach Calvinism will do little to convince a Calvinist that he is wrong. We must seek to understand what Romans 9, John 6, and Ephesians 1 actually teach, not avoid these passages of Scripture. Avoiding election, predestination, and sovereignty will only serve to reinforce the subconscious Calvinist notion that those who reject Calvinism are just rejecting the Bible. However, by providing *biblical* responses to the arguments and proof-texts used by Calvinists, as hopefully this book has accomplished, we at least show that the *only* alternative to Calvinism is *not* the weak, shallow theology of contemporary American Christianity.

Second, we should respond with love, not denigration. Although our opinion is that Calvinism distorts the character of God and undermines the necessity of human responsibility, we do not advocate treating Calvinists with contempt. We are commanded, as followers of Christ, to love our enemies (Matthew 5:44), including our theological "enemies." We should not call Calvinists offensive names for believing Calvinism, even if we think Calvinism damages God's integrity and threatens the holiness of the church. We should speak the truth in love. Our approach ought to be to expose the errors of Calvinism gracefully and to model ourselves after Christ, who was "full of grace and truth" (John 1:14).

BIBLIOGRAPHY

Abasciano, Brian J. "Clearing up Misconceptions about Corporate Election." *Ashland Theological Journal* 41 (2009).

------------. "Corporate Election in Romans 9: A Reply to Thomas Schreiner." *JETS* 49 (2006).

Achtemeier, Paul J. *Romans: Interpretation: A Bible Commentary for Teaching and Preaching.* Louisville: Westminster John Knox Press, 2010.

Allen, David L., Eric Hankins, and Adam Harwood. *Anyone Can Be Saved.* Eugene: Wipf & Stock, 2016.

Allen, David L. *The Extent of the Atonement.* Nashville: B&H Academic, 2016.
----------. "Does Regeneration Precede Faith?" *JBTM* 11:2 (2014).

Allen, David L., and Steve Lemke. *Whosoever Will.* Nashville: B&H Academic, 2010.

Barnes, Albert. *Notes on the New Testament- 1 Corinthians.* Grand Rapids: Baker Book House, 1980.

----------. *Notes On The New Testament- Matthew and Mark.* Grand Rapids: Baker Book House, 1980.

Beilby, James. "Divine Aseity, Divine Freedom: A Conceptual Problem for Edwardsian-Calvinism." *JETS* 47 (2004).

Boettner, Loraine. *The Reformed Doctrine of Predestination*. Phillipsburg: Presbyterian and Reformed Publishing Company, 1932.

Bromiley, Geoffrey W. *Theological Dictionary of the New Testament-Abridged in One Volume*. Grand Rapids: William B. Eerdmans Publishing, 1985.

Brown, Michael. *Hyper-Grace*. Lake Mary: Charisma House, 2014.

Butler, Trent C. *Holman Bible Dictionary*. Nashville: Holman Bible Publishers, 1991.

Calvin, John. *Institutes of the Christian Religion*. Peabody: Hendrickson Publishers, 2008.

Carson, D. A. *The Pillar New Testament Commentary- The Gospel According to John*. Grand Rapids: William B. Eerdmans Company, 1991. Accessed with Logos Bible Software.

Chafer, Lewis Sperry. *Major Bible Themes*. Wheaton: Van Kampen Press, 1953.

Charles, J. Daryl. *Retrieving the Natural Law*. Grand Rapids: Wm. B. Eerdmans, 2008.

Clarke, Adam. *Clarke's Commentary--Volume V.* Nashville: Abingdon, n.d.

Conner, W. T. *The Faith of the New Testament*. Nashville: Broadman Press, 1940.

Dever, Mark. *The Gospel & Personal Evangelism*. Wheaton: Crossway, 2007.

Duffield, Guy, and Nathaniel M. Van Cleave. *Foundations of Pentecostal Theology*. Los Angeles: Foursquare Media, 1987.

Ellicott, Charles J. *Ellicott's Commentary on the Whole Bible – Vol. 7-8*. Grand Rapids: Zondervan Publishing House, 1959.

Elwell, Walter A., ed. *Evangelical Dictionary of Theology*. Grand Rapids: Baker Book House, 1984.

Epp, Theodore H. *Living Abundantly*. Lincoln: Back to the Bible, 1973.

Erickson, Millard J. *Christian Theology- 3rd ed.* Grand Rapids: BakerAcademic, 2013.

Evans, C. Stephens, and R. Zachary Manis. *Philosophy of Religion*. Downers Grove: IVP Academic, 2009.

Fedler, Kyle D. *Exploring Christian Ethics*. Louisville: Westminster John Knox Press, 2006.

Finney, Charles. *Finney's Systematic Theology*. Minneapolis: Bethany House Publishers, 1994.

Fischer, Austin. *Young, Restless, No Longer Reformed*. Eugene: Cascade Books, 2014.

Flowers, Leighton. *The Potter's Promise*. Evansville: Trinity Academic Press, 2017.
-------. "Born Dead?" SOTERIOLOGY 101. April 13, 2018. Accessed May 01, 2019.
https://soteriology101.com/2018/04/13/born-dead/.
-------. "Answering Calvinistic Proof Texts." SOTERIOLOGY 101. October 13, 2016. Accessed May 01, 2019.
https://soteriology101.com/2016/03/16/answering-calvinistic-proof-texts/.

Geisler, Norman. *Chosen But Free*. Minneapolis: Bethany House Publishers, 2010.

--------. *Systematic Theology in One Volume*. Minneapolis: Bethany House, 2011.

Gilbert, Greg. *What Is the Gospel?* Wheaton: Crossway, 2010.

Godet, Frederick L. *Commentary on the Gospel of John- Vol. II*. Grand Rapids: Zondervan, n.d.

Gore, Charles. *The Epistle to the Ephesians*. London: John Murray, Albemarble St., 1898.

Greear, J. D. *Stop Asking Jesus into Your Heart*. Nashville: B&H Academic, 2013.

Grudem, Wayne. *Systematic Theology*. Grand Rapids: Zondervan, 1994.

Hankins, Eric. "Romans 9 and the Calvinist Doctrine of Reprobation." *JBTM* 15 (2018).

Hansen, Collin. *Young, Restless, Reformed*. Wheaton: Crossway, 2008.

Harwood, Adam. "Is the Gospel for All People or Only Some People?" *JBTM* 11 (2014).

Hastings, James, ed. *Encyclopedia of Religion and Ethics*. New York: Charles Scribner's Sons, 1921.

Henry, Carl F. H. *God, Revelation and Authority – Volume V*. Waco: Word Books Publishers, 1982.

Horton, Michael. *For Calvinism*. Grand Rapids: Zondervan, 2011.

Horton, Stanley M. *Systematic Theology*. Springfield: Logion Press, 2003.

Hunt, Dave. *What Love Is This?* Bend: The Berean Call, 2013.

Juncker, Gunther H. "The Dilemma of Theistic Determinism." *Journal for Baptist Theology & Ministry* 12 (2015).

Klein, William. *The New Chosen People.* Eugene: Wipf & Stock, 2015.

Knudsen, Ralph E. *Theology in the New Testament.* Chicago: The Judson Press, 1964.

Lange, John Peter. *Commentary on the Holy Scriptures: Galatians-Colossians.* Grand Rapids: Zondervan Publishing House, n.d.

Lennox, John. *Determined to Believe?* Grand Rapids: Zondervan, 2017.

Longman III, Temper, and David E. Garland. *The Expositor's Bible Commentary-Volume 12.* Grand Rapids: Zondervan, 2006.
--------. *The Expositor's Bible Commentary- Volume 11.* Grand Rapids: Zondervan, 2006.

Lutzer, Erwin. *The Doctrines That Divide.* Grand Rapids: Kregel Publications, 1998.

MacArthur, John. "Coming Alive in Christ." Grace to You. February 26, 1978. Accessed May 01, 2019. https://www.gty.org/library/sermons-library/1908/coming-alive-in-christ.

Marshall, I. Howard. *Kept by the Power of God.* Eugene: Wipf & Stock Publishers, 2007.

Marston, Paul, and Roger Forster. *God's Strategy in Human History.* Eugene: Wipf & Stock, 2000.

Martin, Earl. *Toward Understanding God.* Anderson: Gospel Trumpet Company, 1942.

McCall, Tom. "We Believe in God's Sovereign Goodness." *Trinity Journal* 29 (2008).

---------. "I Believe in Divine Sovereignty." *Trinity Journal* 29 (2008).

Meister, Chad, and James K. Dew Jr. *God and Evil*. Downers Grove: InterVarsity Press, 2013.

Miley, John. *Systematic Theology- Vol. 2*. Peabody: Hendrickson Publishers, 1989.

Moody, Dale. *The Word of Truth*. Grand Rapids: Wm. B. Eerdmans Publishing, 1981.

Morris, Leon. *Tyndale New Testament Commentaries- 1 Corinthians*. Grand Rapids: Wm. B. Eerdmans Publishing, 1987.

Newman, Carey C. "Election and Predestination in Ephesians 1:4-6a: An Exegetical-Theological Study of the Historical, Christological Realization of God's Purpose." *Review and Expositor* 93 (1996).

Nicoll, W. Robertson. *The Expositor's Bible: The Epistle to the Ephesians*. New York: George H. Doran Company, n.d.

Ockenga, Harold J. *Faithful in Christ Jesus*. New York: Fleming H. Revell Company, 1948.

Oden, Thomas C. *The Living God-Systematic Theology-Volume One*. San Francisco: HarperCollins Publishers, 1987.

-------. *The Transforming Power of Grace*. Nashville: Abingdon Press, 1993.

Olson, Roger. *Against Calvinism*. Grand Rapids: Zondervan, 2011.

-------. *Arminian Theology: Myths and Realities*. Downers Grove, IL: IVP Academic, 2006.

Pearlman, Myer. *Knowing the Doctrines of the Bible*. Springfield: Gospel Publishing House, 1937.

Peckham, John C. *The Love of God*. Downers Grove: IVP Academic, 2015.

Picirilli, Robert. *Grace, Faith, Free Will*. Nashville: Randall House, 2002.

Pink, Arthur W. *The Sovereignty of God*. London: Banner of Truth, 1968.

Piper, John. "What We Believe About the Five Points of Calvinism." Desiring God. May 01, 2019. Accessed May 01, 2019. https://www.desiringgod.org/articles/what-we-believe-about-the-five-points-of-calvinism#Grace.

Purkiser, W. T., Richard S. Taylor, and Willard H. Taylor. *God, Man, & Salvation*. Kansas City: Beacon Hill Press, 1977.

Robertson, A.T. *Word Pictures in the New Testament* Vol. IV. Nashville: Broadman Press, 1931.

Ross, Allen. *Creation & Blessing*. Grand Rapids: Baker Academic, 1997.

Sailer, William. "The Nature and Extent of the Atonement- A Wesleyan View." *Bulletin of the Evangelical Theological Society* 10 (1967).

Shank, Robert. *Life in the Son*. Springfield: Westcott House, 1961.
--------. *Elect in the Son*. Minneapolis: Bethany House Publishers, 1989.

Shellrude, Glen. "The freedom of God in mercy and judgment: a libertarian reading of Romans 9:6-29." *EQ* 81 (2009).

Sproul, R. C. *Chosen by God*. Carol Stream: Tyndale House Publishers, 1986.

--------. *What is Reformed Theology?* Grand Rapids: BakerBooks, 1997.

Stagg, Frank. *New Testament Theology*. Nashville: Broadman Press, 1962.

Steele, David N., and Curtis Thomas. *The Five Points of Calvinism*. Phillipsburg: Presbyterian & Reformed Publishing Co., 1963.

Taylor, John W. "The Freedom of God and the Hope of Israel: Theological Interpretation of Romans." *Southwestern Journal of Theology* 56 (2013).

Taylor, Richard. *Leading Wesleyan Thinkers- Volume 3*. Kansas City: Beacon Hill Press, n.d.

Thayer, Joseph H. *Thayer's Greek-English Lexicon of the New Testament*. Peabody: Hendrickson Publishers, 2000.

Thiessen, H. C. *Introductory Lectures in Systematic Theology*. Grand Rapids: Wm. B. Eerdmans Publishing Company, 1977.

Tillett, Wilbur. *Personal Salvation*. Nashville: Publishing House of the M.E. Church, South, 1902.

Trimm, Charlie. "Did YHWH Condemn the Nations When He Elected Israel? YHWH's Disposition toward Non-Israelites in the Torah." *JETS* 55 (2012).

Unger, Merrill F. *Unger's Bible Dictionary*. Chicago: Moody Press, 1966.

Vine, W. E. *Vine's Complete Expository Dictionary of Old and New Testament Words*. Nashville: Thomas Nelson Publishers, 1996.

Walls, Jerry L., and Joseph R. Dongell. *Why I Am Not a Calvinist.* Downers Grove: InterVarsity Press, 2004.

Walls, Jerry. "Why No Classical Theist, Let Alone Orthodox Christian, Should Ever Be a Compatibilist." *Philosophia Christi* 13 (2011).
-------. *Does God Love Everyone?* Eugene: Cascade Books, 2016.

Wesley, John. *The Works of John Wesley- Vol. X.* Grand Rapids: Baker Book House, 1978.

White, James. *The Potter's Freedom.* Calvary Publishing Press, 2009.

Wilkin, Jen. *None Like Him.* Wheaton: Crossway, 2016.

Witherington III, Ben. *The Problem with Evangelical Theology.* Waco: Baylor University Press, 2005.
--------. *John's Wisdom.* Louisville: Westminster John Knox Press, 1995.
--------. *Paul's Letter to the Romans.* Grand Rapids: Wm. B. Eerdmans, 2004.

GLOSSARY

1. **Antinomianism-** the belief that Christians are not bound to obedience to the moral law
2. **Apologetics-** a reasonable defense of the Christian faith
3. **Apostasy-** the act of departing from a saving relationship with Jesus Christ
4. **Apostles-** the twelve men Jesus Christ chose out of his disciples
5. **Application of the atonement-** refers to when the atonement is applied to the sinner
6. **Aseity-** God is eternally self-existent in and of Himself
7. **Assurance-** the knowledge that a Christian can possess whereby he knows that he is saved
8. **Atonement-** Jesus' sacrificial death for the sins of the world
9. **Attributes-** a term that theologians often use in reference to different aspects of God's nature, such as love, holiness, sovereignty, and knowledge
10. **Calvinism-** a theological system, named after sixteenth-century French Reformer, that is frequently summarized in the acronym TULIP
11. **Cessationism-** the belief that the spiritual gifts ceased in the apostolic age
12. **Compatibilism-** the view that determinism and free will are compatible. In this system, free will is defined as the ability to do what we want to do
13. **Context-** the background to any passage under consideration

14. **Decree-** a term used by Calvinists to describe God's immutable decision of everything that comes to pass
15. **Doctrine-** any belief taught in the Scriptures
16. **Eisegesis-** reading into the Bible a meaning that is foreign to the passage
17. **Salvific election-** God's sovereign choice, before the beginning of time, of those who are in Christ for salvation
18. **Eternal life-** the life only found in a relationship with God through the Lord Jesus Christ
19. **Exegesis-** drawing out of the Bible its intended meaning
20. **Extent of the atonement-** addresses the topic of who Christ died for
21. **Faith-** an acceptance of the truth about Christ and a trusting in him and his finished work for sin
22. **Fall-** a term that refers to the entrance of sin into the world through the disobedience of Adam
23. **Foreknowledge-** God's knowledge of the future
24. **Hermeneutics-** the science of biblical interpretation
25. **Immutability-** an attribute of God which indicates that he does not change
26. **Incarnation-** when God became man in the person of Jesus
27. **Intent of the atonement-** deals with the question of what God designed the atonement for
28. **Irresistible grace-** a Calvinistic term that refers to God's action of changing the disposition of a fallen person's heart so that he will come to Christ in faith
29. **Libertarian free will-** the view that human beings have the power of contrary choice
30. **Limited atonement-** the view that Jesus died only for the sins of the elect
31. **Monergism-** salvation is accomplished by God alone, not dependent on any action of the individual
32. **Omniscient-** God knows all things
33. **Ordo salutis-** the order of salvation
34. **Patristic-** the era of the early church fathers

35. **Perseverance of the Saints-** the view that the elect will necessarily persevere in faith until the end

36. **Predestination-** God's determination of certain ends, such as conformity to Christ's image and adoption as sons, for those who are in Christ

37. **Presupposition**s- these are beliefs people hold subconsciously that affect their interpretation and dictate their conclusions

38. **Proof-texting-** this occurs when an individual defends his theological position by quoting a verse out of context to support his position even though the verse doesn't really support his position

39. **Pure actuality-** God has no potential to not exist and is the uncaused Cause of all that began to exist

40. **Reformed theology-** generally a synonym for Calvinism, although this is somewhat inaccurate

41. **Regeneration-** the new birth that occurs at salvation when a sinner has faith in God and turns to him in repentance

42. **Repentance-** a change of mind about sin and God that results in a change of action, accompanied by an intense remorse for previous iniquities

43. **Reprobation-** the necessary corollary to unconditional election. Because God has chosen certain people for eternal salvation, those not chosen are destined for eternal perdition.

44. **Soteriology-** the doctrine of salvation

45. **Sovereignty-** God is in control of all creation

46. **Spiritual death-** to be alienated from a relationship with God, not to be as unresponsive as a corpse

47. **Synergism-** God saves people in response to their faith and repentance

48. **Theology-** the study of God

49. **Theistic determinism (also divine determinism)-** God has determined everything that comes, or will come, to pass, including sin, evil, and natural disasters

50. **Total depravity-** in relation to Calvinism, this term describes fallen man's inability to respond to God's grace. This is because of the radical corruption that resulted from the fall.

51. **TULIP-** an acronym that stands for the five points of Calvinism: total depravity, unconditional election, limited atonement, irresistible grace, and the perseverance of the saints

52. **Unconditional election-** the view that God has chosen a group of individuals, known as the elect, for salvation. He did this irrespective of their good works or faith.

53. **Unlimited atonement-** the belief that Jesus Christ died for the sins of everyone

54. **Universalism-** the view that, in the final analysis, everyone will be saved

55. **Vocational election-** God's choice of certain groups or individuals to play a specific task in human history

56. **Wills of God-** Calvinists teach that God has two wills: a secret will and a revealed will. God's secret will refers to that which will necessarily come to pass, just as he has decreed. His revealed will, on the other hand, is his desires that are expressed in the Scriptures